HOLY GRIT

"Living in a world where, in some circles, the word 'masculinity' is an offensive word, Paul George does a wonderful job exploring what it means to be a man, a man of holy grit. George doesn't look to professional athletes or superheroes, but rather to men who have 'run the race well'—men of faith who have gone before us. I so appreciate George's honesty and vulnerability. He shares his struggles and triumphs in a way that will be accessible to a wide range of men. Whether you are young, older, a father, or a son, you will find George's stories engaging and helpful. I have been blessed to walk with George on his journey of faith for more than twenty-five years. I've appreciated him as a brother and have been inspired by his example of a man after God's heart. As you journey with George in search of holy grit, there's no doubt in my mind you too will be blessed."

Fr. Dave Pivonka, TOR
President of Franciscan University of Steubenville

"More than talent or IQ, grit may be the greatest determinant of human achievement. God is beckoning us to seize the day, to be about the Father's business with passion and perseverance. Awake, O sleeper, rise and grind! Yet in the spiritual life, our own efforts are simply not enough. The title says it all—*Holy Grit*! I dream of the marvels God can accomplish through gritty men who allow his holy grace to take hold of their lives! Grab this book, roll up your sleeves, and surrender."

Mark Hartfiel
Vice President of *Paradisus Dei*/That Man Is You

"A timely book for all faithful sons of Holy Mother Church striving to stay on the narrow way. This book is a must-read for all men who take their faith seriously and are looking to apply and expand their level of grit practically in their daily lives. It is an unapologetic, hard-hitting topic for men of all seasons seeking to understand grit using time-tested principles drawn from the wisdom of Catholic saints. Look no further if you want inspiration and practical steps to become the true man and saint God is calling you to be! Read this book."

Samuel H. Blair
Cofounder of The Frassati Company

"What does it mean to be a real man? Is John Wayne (in the movie *True Grit*) the prototype of authentic masculinity? Or is all masculinity toxic—as our modern culture claims? In this book, Paul George masterfully proposes an age-old vision of masculinity. He calls it 'holy grit.' Drawing out the masculine genius through the personal stories of some of our favorite saints down through the ages (Joseph, Peter, Paul, Augustine, St. Ignatius of Loyola, Thomas More, Louis Martin, Maximillian Kolbe, Padre Pio, and John Paul II), he weaves in his own story throughout each chapter to show how healing is essential for us to live in the freedom of our manhood. I highly recommend this book to all men, and for women who long to encourage their husbands, fathers, and brothers to live from their hearts with tender strength."

Bob Schuchts
Founder of the John Paul II Healing Center

"Drawing from the sacred scriptures, the *Catechism of the Catholic Church*, the lives of the saints, and his personal experiences, Paul George aims to inspire men in their relationship with God and equip them with tools that can help them live integrated lives as healthy, holy, and mature disciples of Jesus Christ in their family, in the Church, and in the world."

Fr. Josh Johnson
Director of vocations for the Diocese of Baton Rouge and
host of *Ask Father Josh*

"If there's one person I know who has the moral authority to teach on what it is to be a true man of God, it's Paul George. In this book, George has summarized and communicated what has cost him his entire life to learn and achieve: what holy grit is and how to become a man after God's own heart."

Fr. Mike Schmitz
Host of the *Bible in a Year* podcast

"*Holy Grit* does an incredible job of using the power of story-telling to inspire a generation of men to become who God is calling them to be. I found myself laughing along and relating to his stories while also being challenged to grow in virtue. I particularly enjoyed the action plans at the end of each chapter as they allow the book to be implemented over a period of time to have a lasting effect on the reader. I will be sharing this with the men in my community."

Jonathan "Bearded" Blevins
Founder of Little Flower Media

HOLY GRIT

A SAINTLY GUIDE TO BECOMING A MAN OF VIRTUE

PAUL GEORGE

AVE MARIA PRESS AVE Notre Dame, Indiana

© 2023 by Paul George

All rights reserved. No part of this book may be used or reproduced in any manner whatsoever, except in the case of reprints in the context of reviews, without written permission from Ave Maria Press®, Inc., P.O. Box 428, Notre Dame, IN 46556, 1-800-282-1865.

Founded in 1865, Ave Maria Press is a ministry of the United States Province of Holy Cross.

www.avemariapress.com

Paperback: ISBN-13 978-1-64680-198-5

E-book: ISBN-13 978-1-64680-199-2

Cover image © Getty Images.

Cover and text design by Andy Wagoner.

Printed and bound in the United States of America.

Library of Congress Cataloging-in-Publication Data is available.

DEDICATED TO

Sam George and Sam Jacobs, and to all the gritty and holy men, sinners and saints alike, who have impacted my life.

THANKS TO

Gretchen, Marie, Jacob, Sarah, Clare, Addie, Mom and Dad.

CONTENTS

INTRODUCTION

If you are like me, you appreciate buckling up and addressing issues head-on. I'm sure you also appreciate honesty, boldness, and truth. I promise that this book will not waste your time or water things down; we don't have time for that. In these pages, we will look at some of the tough issues facing men—our struggles in marriage, parenting, discernment, suffering, purpose, trusting God, and finding peace in our identity as his sons. Together, we will take a hard look at our lives, especially the areas where we need growth, and identify steps for moving into the joy-filled life we all desire. This book won't answer all your questions, but it will boost you to move ahead, to press on and embrace the life God created you for, just as the saints I talk about in these pages did.

I can recall vivid images from my childhood of men who were tough. Even today those images are stuck in my mind. Some of those men were real-life sports heroes, while others were in movies or TV shows. But they all had one thing in common—those men had *grit*! They were tough men—men who knocked out their opponent in a boxing ring, took a hockey puck to the teeth, had the fastest gun in a Wild West shootout, flew a fighter jet, fled from the police in a fancy car, played a football game with a broken rib, or slid into second base headfirst, taking a spike to the nose. I loved those guys, and I wanted to be a man like them.

I grew up in the country. Many kids from my generation played cowboys and Indians, dreaming of what it would be like to be tough and gritty. My grandfather Sam didn't play the role of a cowboy; he was one, literally. Anyone who knew him had a story about Sam George. Even today, I meet people who have stories about my grandfather, whom I called "Pappy." He was one of a kind—a dying breed, as many would say.

During most of my childhood, Pappy was more of a figure to me than a person. I seldom saw him, and the few words he spoke to me as a kid (he passed away when I was nineteen) I can't repeat in this book. He was special, if flawed, and I loved him despite his rough ways. I remember one occasion when my dad and I went to visit him. He was working cattle and rode up on his horse. He looked at me (I could barely see his squinty eyes beneath the rim of his cowboy hat) and asked what I had been up to. I said, "Hey Pappy, I'm playing tackle football!" I was in fifth grade and had made the sixth and seventh grade squad. I had just played in a game the day before and was proud of my bruises. He responded, "Football is for —— [wimps]. Real men ride horses and bulls!" That statement stuck with me. I began to wonder what it was like to be a "real man," one who proved his masculinity by showing others how tough he was. I wanted to be a man with grit! Who doesn't?

An online dictionary defines "grit" as "firmness of character; indomitable spirit; pluck." Synonyms include "backbone, daring, doggedness, fortitude, gameness, guts, hardihood, boldness, courageousness, intestinal fortitude, mettle, moxie, nerve, perseverance, resolution, spine, spirit, and spunk." Every one of these words is what every man, myself included, wants to be known for. All of us want to have moxie, spine, spunk! We are built for grit. I admit that if someone were to describe me, I'd want the word "grit" in the description.

However, grit alone will not and cannot satisfy our masculine souls. We can't "grit" our way through life. Trust me, I've tried and failed. In my work as a spiritual life coach, speaker, and consultant, I've had the privilege of talking to hundreds of men, many of whom have grit. Grit alone failed them, too. A man can ride horses and bulls, like Pappy, but that will never totally satisfy what he really desires. We are made for more than just grit. We are made for *holy grit*.

We all have our own unique story, the story that got us to where we are today. I'm the first to admit that my story isn't perfect. It is riddled with mistakes, regrets, and wrong turns. I worry and stress too much. The good news is that this book isn't about being perfect, and it's not about being a "real man."

As I set out on this project, I found myself wondering, Who am I to write a book for men? I'm not an expert, though there are plenty of those out there if you are looking for them. I'm a man, just like you, on a journey. On my journey, I have been fortunate to encounter God, his healing, and his grace. I have seen the effects of these gifts play out in my story. I have also encountered great men who have shown me the path to follow—a path of true peace and joy, a path that leads to a life of not only grit, but also holiness. It is these men, the men in sacred scripture and other saints, who have inspired this book. These are the men I want to be like.

What does it mean to have holy grit? How do holiness and grittiness work together? What do the saints show us about this? What does Jesus teach us about being a man? How does a life of holiness affect our work, marriage, family, and friendships? These are all questions we will tackle in this book. We will look at the lives of gritty saints who show us what manhood can and should be.

In these pages we won't shy away from the tough words, hard teachings, and bold statements of men with holy grit who have gone before us. I fully believe that you, as men, are ready to embrace whatever is in front of you, and with God's grace you can walk through anything.

Let's get to it! Together, man-to-man.

1

LET'S BE FRANK

Saying yes to God with St. Joseph

Joseph is one of the greatest figures in Christianity. We know little about him, yet he changed the course of history. Joseph was the son of Jacob, the husband of Mary, and the earthly father of Jesus, the Messiah. Some historians date Joseph's birth around 90 BC and his death around AD 18.

Joseph's lineage can be traced back to the great king David, an important fact in salvation history. We first hear of Joseph in the Gospels of Matthew and Luke. We know little about Joseph from scripture, but what we do know is very telling.

Joseph worked with his hands, probably taught by his father Jacob. We know he was a carpenter, for the skeptical Nazarenes ask about Jesus, "Is he not the carpenter's son?" (Mt 13:55). The Greek word usually translated as "carpenter" today can also refer more generally to a craftsman or to one who works with both wood and stone. So it's possible that Joseph was a stone mason as well. We know Joseph wasn't rich, for when he and Mary took Jesus to the Temple to be circumcised, they offered the sacrifice of two turtledoves or a pair of pigeons, allowed only for those who could not afford a lamb (see Luke 2:24).

Jesus would have learned his trade by working alongside Joseph, watching him as a young child and then learning hands-on. Joseph was a provider, a husband, and a dad. He was a man of grit, who taught his son to be tough as well.

I've always loved working with my hands, getting dirty. I have admired guys like Joseph, who day-to-day make a living doing physical labor. One of my friends' dads was a carpenter. His hands were always cracked, calloused, and swollen. Hands of a gritty man, and I admired that. Joseph's hands were probably worn and calloused, too. He was a man with grit.

I imagine that Joseph was a hard worker—an average man, like you and me, who made a living and maybe saved a little for the future. He was probably content with his life and work and at some point began to desire a family. According to Jewish tradition of the time, Joseph's marriage to Mary would probably have been arranged by their families. We aren't sure how old Joseph and Mary were when they were betrothed, but many theologians suggest that Mary was a young teenager and Joseph was years older. I'm certain that Joseph had plans for the future with his beautiful wife and their family, just like everyone else who has ever been engaged and dreamed of an amazing, joy-filled life with the one they love.

Joseph's plans changed when he discovered that his fiancée was pregnant, and that the child she carried was not his. His dreams came to a halt. Imagine the confusion and stress Joseph must have experienced. He was in a bind. He needed to make a decision before everyone else found out! The Gospel of Matthew states that when Mary "was found with child through the holy Spirit[,] Joseph her husband, since he was a righteous man, yet unwilling to expose her to shame, decided to divorce her quietly" (1:18–19).

Joseph was a "righteous" man, that is, a godly man who was "right with" God. His heart was good, and he desired to do the right thing. We can relate to this. You and I, in our hearts, want to do what's right and what is good. And we all know, like Joseph, what it's like to face tough decisions.

We can also see that Joseph was a work in progress—that he was human, like me and you. He didn't have it all figured out. He didn't have it all together; he was not perfect. He was upset, confused, and searching for answers during a stressful time. His immediate decision was to eject from the situation, disappear, move on. If he left, the problem would go away, right?

The urge for Joseph to deflect, eject, and ignore the situation must have been strong. I can relate, yet I can't imagine what Joseph was going through. He made up his mind to end the engagement quietly, letting Mary tend to her mess alone. Leaving her quietly, not exposing her to public shame, made his conscience feel good. He was doing a good thing, and probably reasoned to himself, *I'll do what I can, the minimum that's required of me to be a good and righteous man.* Isn't that the baseline standard for men—to be a "good person"? I hear this often in my conversations with other men: "I'm a good man." Joseph could leave and move on, forget about the past, and pretend all was well. That's what men with grit do, they pick themselves up by the bootstraps and move on!

I can relate to Joseph in this situation as a man and a husband. I can sense his anxiety, the pressure to make the right decision and do the right thing. Leaving Mary made sense. Why? Because it was justified. This was not his problem to solve, right? Adultery (which Joseph assumed had occurred) was a grave offense, even meriting being stoned to death. So Joseph would not bring Mary to public shame. But he felt justified in leaving her.

That's how I feel when someone confronts me about my behavior. When I'm wrong, I want to justify my feelings and behavior. I want to justify my decisions because I've been wronged, so now I deserve to act out of my hurt. Joseph felt he was wronged and thus justified in his decision. He was hurt. And when people are hurt, they hurt other people!

Justification is a slippery slope, because justice without love, mercy, understanding, and wisdom can steer us off the road. Unchecked justice usually leads to self-gratification, what's best for me. I'm right, you're wrong; you deserve what's coming to you.

I'm not saying that justice isn't important. It is, but it's not the only virtue to help us make a good decision. The greatest virtue isn't justice, it's love. St. Paul tells us, "So faith, hope, love remain, these three; but the greatest of these is love" (1 Cor 13:13). Being just takes grit; but being kind, forgiving, loving, and discerning takes more than grit, it takes *holy grit*.

Joseph needed help with his decision. I'm certain that before he slept on his plan, he prayed for guidance. His desire to do the right thing and his heart tuned to righteousness were all God needed to intervene. God always desires to help us in our doubt. He brings light to our darkness and clears the fog when we can't see clearly.

God intervened in Joseph's heart in his time of distress, as the Gospel of Matthew tells us: "Such was his intention when, behold, the angel of the Lord appeared to him in a dream and said, 'Joseph, son of David, do not be afraid to take Mary your wife into your home. For it is through the holy Spirit that this child has been conceived in her'" (1:20). God had spoken.

God speaks to our hearts too, but do we listen? The same God that spoke to Joseph through a dream is the God who speaks to us today. In stillness and quiet, God speaks. In the midst of storms, God is present. The same grace that Joseph received is the grace we received through baptism and that remains with us today. God is near, always.

The course of Joseph's life changed the day he said yes to God's plan. It wasn't the route he had chosen, but he would come to see that God's plan was much better than his own. Grit by itself would have left him justified, but probably divorced and alone. His holy grit, achieved through God's grace, gave him an amazing wife and son to love and care for. Imagine missing out on the joy of the Holy Family.

Scripture tells us of a few other times when Joseph demonstrated his willingness to follow God's plan rather than his own. When God directed him to a manger in Bethlehem when Mary was ready to give birth, Joseph was obedient. When God told him to evacuate to Egypt in the middle of the night to escape the imminent slaughter of the Child Jesus, Joseph did it. When it was time to return to Nazareth to raise his family and to work, Joseph went to Nazareth.

To this day, many men have looked to Joseph for guidance. Saints throughout history have prayed to Joseph. Joseph is a model for us as men—a model of faith, obedience, and trust. He chose to grow in holiness. He chose to say yes to God's plan. He chose to move from being gritty to being holy, too. He will forever be a man of holy grit. For all of eternity, he will be revered as a great saint, St. Joseph the Worker.

CONFRONTING OURSELVES

One day during my first semester in college, I found myself face-to-face with my baseball coach in the dugout. He was direct with me about my subpar play. In short, he let me know that I was probably *not* going to see the field much during the upcoming season. I was devastated and angry. This was not how I envisioned my life's plan unfolding. It took courage for my coach to be frank with me, but that honesty was difficult for me to receive. My identity was in what I did and what I accomplished. Who was I without it?

That incident made me question myself and began to change the direction of my life. Looking back, I can see it was a St. Joseph moment for me. All of a sudden I had come to a fork in the road. My plans did not match up with God's plans, and I needed help, intervention. That help did not come immediately, but the incident did move my heart to realize that my life and my identity were more about who I was than what I did.

I've been on the receiving end of many conversations like this. Not all of them involved major issues that required major attention. Some were simple opportunities for humility and growth. But some gave me the opportunity to confront hard truths.

I remember a conversation with my wife, Gretchen, about my years of manic behavior around the holidays. She was honest with me about her observations. She asked that I look at this issue and figure out how, with God's help, I could change it. I was not happy with her, and I wanted to point the finger back, pass the blame to her and to everyone and everything else for my behavior. As I thought about it, however, I realized that she was right; this was my issue to work through, one that affected not only me, but my family too.

It was an issue with a deep backstory. Sadness would rise up in me during the holidays as I remembered my parents' divorce and the absence we all felt as a divided family during the "happy holidays." Before my eighth Christmas, holidays were like going to Disney World. We spent Christmas Eve at my grandparents' house with our cousins and aunts and uncles, unwrapping what seemed like hundreds of gifts. On Christmas morning my sister and I would walk into the living room, at the only house we'd ever lived in, and it would be filled with presents, laughter, and joy. After the divorce, everything changed. We spent Christmas mornings in another house in another town with my mom. Afternoons were at my dad's house in the town where I was born, and it was different. I had lost a lot—my happy childhood, my hometown, our family being together laughing and enjoying the holidays.

As an adult, I tried to pretend that I was okay during the holidays, but memories surfaced and made me angry and sad. I thought to myself, *I'm all right, I should be able to fake my way through this.* But the memories made me Scrooge-like and difficult to be around. My wife finally had enough and confronted me with a frank talk about my behavior. We had children; did I want to carry this anger and sadness into their lives, especially around Christmastime?

I didn't want to look at the past, I wanted to forget about it. Like men of grit, I wanted to just "move on." I felt justified in my feelings. But justification alone is not enough. Like Joseph, I needed to find love, mercy, understanding, and wisdom. Grit without God wasn't enough; at least for me it wasn't.

I learned from this episode that pain doesn't go away unless we meet it face-to-face, man-to-man. So I faced it. I worked through it. I got help. I talked to someone. I prayed, healed, and grew a lot. The journey continues, but it's a good one, a healing one.

Grit involves staying the course, perhaps hoping that God will clear the air and our problems will go away. *Holy grit*, on the other hand, involves a willingness to turn around and reroute our course—to listen to God and respond. Holy grit is facing things head-on, with God leading the way. Men who seek God do not move on until God has done his work. They stay, face the challenge, and, like St. Joseph, say yes to God.

Scripture tells us, "When Joseph awoke, he did as the angel of the Lord had commanded him and took his wife into his home" (Mt 1:24). Despite the dictates of the law, despite pressure from society, despite his human desire to leave Mary, despite what was justified, Joseph did the right thing, the holy thing. His total yes to God, despite the difficulty ahead, was where he found true freedom.

We all have hurts from our past. We've all made mistakes and have regrets. These things don't define us, but they can affect our lives and the lives of those we love if we don't work through them.

Men appreciate honesty—the facts. We like the truth, the bold truth. We don't want someone to water things down, to be reticent in their communication, or not say what's on their mind. Except, of course, when it is directed at us and our shortcomings. I admit that when someone is frank with me about my behavior, I don't like it, but most times I need to hear it. Often when it comes to the truth about our lives, we men tend to deflect, eject, or ignore. That's what happened when Gretchen confronted me about my behavior around the holidays. I wanted to dodge the issue, distance myself from the truth of her words.

Some of us are great at deflecting. We quickly pass the blame on to something or someone else. We laugh it off, make a joke. We may accuse someone else and make them feel like they are the problem. We may make excuses about all the things that are not going our way. It's difficult to accept blame. We'd rather pretend we are strong and have it all together than to be humble and admit our weakness.

Some of us eject from the issue. Like a fighter pilot going down, we pull the cord and leap from the plane because an engine failed. Abort mission! What we should do is stay in the plane, correct course, and land. It's amazing how some of us can face a crisis at work or a challenge on the field or court, yet when it comes to personal issues, we would rather hide in an emotional foxhole. A small disagreement with your wife can spiral into an emotional dilemma that you can't get out of fast enough. Pull the cord, get out quickly, before I discover that I'm wrong!

Some of us are experts at ignoring the issue. We may pretend all is well. Out of sight, out of mind is our motto. We are good at forgetting, unless we need to hold a grudge to make us feel better. We compartmentalize. Our mind has nice, neat boxes where we store things. However, issues don't go away. They linger nearby until we deal with them. Things that we thought were tucked away neatly begin to spill over into other boxes!

I say all this because I've walked this journey. I've deflected, ejected, and ignored issues many times. Being buried under the weight of what we choose not to deal with, lying in a foxhole alone, is an exhausting way to live. The reality is that the sun will come out from behind the clouds. Our desire to heal and be well will bear fruit—but only if we are honest and live in God's truth. Honesty and truth can set us free from our old ways of thinking, giving new vision to our shortsightedness. Jesus states clearly, "If you remain in my word, you will truly be my disciples, and you will know the truth, and the truth will set you free" (Jn 8:31–32).

Grit alone can't save us, but growing in truth, honesty, and holiness, and allowing the grace of Christ to transform us, can. Saying yes to God isn't always easy, but it's where we find freedom. I've seen it firsthand in my own life and in the lives of other men. The lives of the saints give ample evidence of this truth. St. Joseph in particular shows us how to say yes to God and to find freedom in following God's plan.

AN INVITATION

Men are made to be heroic. It's in our nature to stand up, fight, and defend—to run into a burning building to save those who are left behind. But heroes aren't created overnight. They are sculpted over time, chiseled carefully, and sometimes need to be broken and remade before their best qualities show forth. That's all of us, being made and remade.

When I decided to lean in to Gretchen's frank assessment of my behavior, I took time to really reflect. I asked for the grace to accept her feedback. I prayed and talked with someone about it. I was open, like Joseph, to my heart changing, and over time, it did.

God said to the prophet Jeremiah: "Arise and go down to the potter's house; there you will hear my word. I went down to the potter's house and there he was, working at the wheel" (18:2–3). The potter represents God the Father. When Jeremiah saw the potter working, molding and shaping the clay, he was mesmerized by the potter's attention to detail. This was the potter's art, his joy. The passage continues: "Whenever the vessel of clay he was making turned out badly in his hand, he tried again, making another vessel of whatever sort he pleased" (18:4). Jeremiah was puzzled by this. The vessel was turning out badly; something didn't look right. Jeremiah thought as you and I would, that the potter should throw the vessel away and start over. Nope. That's not what the potter did. His mission was to make the clay into something beautiful, and he knew that would take time, patience, and love. So "he tried again." This is what God did with St. Joseph's heart and plans, and look how it turned out. He wants to do that with us as well.

God is extremely patient and loving with us. Like the potter, he doesn't throw us away. Despite our flaws, God puts us back on the wheel and reshapes us, making us into the men he desires us to be. This reshaping and remaking can be painful and time-consuming. But when we allow ourselves to be reworked in God's hands, we become who we were meant to be. This is where it begins and where it ends. You and me, in his hands.

Maybe your life needs some reshaping. Maybe you simply need a reminder. Maybe you think you aren't good enough. Maybe you dream of living a life other than your own. Maybe you feel distant from God. Maybe you are exhausted. Maybe you are scared. Maybe you live in a house full of people and yet you are lonely. Maybe your heart is broken. Maybe you're looking for a boost in your spiritual life. Maybe you're out of gritty options and need godly ones. I've been in all of these places.

I love the words of Peter in the Gospel of John when things were getting hard and Jesus asked the apostles if they wanted to quit. Peter said, "Master, to whom shall we go? You have the words of eternal life" (6:68). Our lives, like St. Joseph's, begin to make sense when we give our total yes to God, when we go to him to restore our lives and our hearts. Our world, our towns, our neighborhoods need men who, like St. Joseph, are willing to be heroic in their yes to the Lord each day. To be men of holy grit.

I invite you to allow God to meet you right where you are, as he did with St. Joseph. To take the step forward in giving your total yes to God.

St. Joseph, pray for us!

ACTION PLAN

1. Be open. Ask God for the grace to be honest with yourself about your life. Where are you emotionally and spiritually in your journey? What areas of your life need attention?

2. Take some time to:
   o Pray about these things.

○   Go to Confession and receive the Sacrament of
     Reconciliation.

○   Talk to someone about what you have reflected on—a
     friend, mentor, spiritual director, or counselor.

Prayer to St. Joseph

O St. Joseph, whose protection is so great, so prompt, so
strong, before the throne of God, I place in you all my inter-
ests and desires. O St. Joseph, do assist me by your powerful intercession, and obtain for me from your divine Son all
spiritual blessings, through Jesus Christ, our Lord. So that,
having engaged here below your heavenly power, I may offer
my thanksgiving and homage to the most loving of fathers. O
St. Joseph, I never weary contemplating you and Jesus asleep
in your arms; I dare not approach while he reposes near your
heart. Press him in my name and kiss his fine head for me
and ask him to return the kiss when I draw my dying breath.
Amen.

DISCUSSION/JOURNALING QUESTIONS

1. How would you describe your relationship with Christ
    right now? In what ways do you see potential to grow
    spiritually?

2. Look honestly at your life as a man, friend, husband, and/
    or father. What are potential areas for growth? In what
    way do you need God to reshape you?

3. How do you see St. Joseph as a model for yourself and
    your life?

4. What do you need prayers for the most right now in your life?

2

THE FOUR B'S

Overcoming obstacles with St. Augustine

Augustine was born on November 13, 354, in what is now known as Algeria. His parents were both influential in his life. Augustine's father, Patricius, was educated and well loved. He worked as a city official—a politician of sorts. Patricius was a pagan, and these two factors, education and unbelief, were key motivators early in Augustine's life.

Augustine's mother, Monica, was a strong, humble, and prayerful woman. She was committed to raising Augustine and his siblings in a Christian home. She insisted, even though her husband was not a believer, that Augustine receive a Christian education. Monica never relented in her love, encouragement, and pursuit of her son's heart and faith.

Augustine had an active intellect and a drive to succeed. By the age of sixteen he moved away from home to study rhetoric. His hunger for knowledge and his desire to achieve drove Augustine up the ladder of success. His speaking skills earned him recognition and promotion, so that he became one of the best orators around. Augustine had grit. He was tough, both intellectually and physically.

Yet Augustine's heart also longed for more than worldly accomplishments. Just like me and you, he desired fulfillment, the kind of fulfillment that knowledge, education, and success could not satisfy. One of Augustine's best-known quotes, "Thou hast created us for thyself, and our heart is not quiet until it rests in thee," gives us insight into his longing for spiritual fulfillment. This quote from Augustine's *Confessions* has personally captured me for years. I've used it in talks, I've given it to others. It's what I long for too—to find rest and peace in God.

Augustine lived a life of lust and debauchery. He sought out power, achievement, and money. As men, we can relate to Augustine. We all know what it's like to try to find fulfillment in something other than God. We know what it's like to seek and not find, to try to fill a void that only God can fill, with something temporal.

While living in Carthage, Augustine fathered a son (Adeodatus) with his mistress. He took ownership of his actions by accepting responsibility for his child. This is what men of grit do; they take responsibility for their choices, good and bad. But those choices have lasting consequences.

In his writings, Augustine documents his past mistakes. It is clear that at this point in his life he had grit but was not yet holy. His grit led him to seek power, control, money, fame, popularity. He used women, booze, and an assortment of vices to fill the void deep in his soul. He also used his knowledge and intellect to lord it over others. Grit without God could sum up the first half of Augustine's life.

It was during this time far from God, a time of deep desolation, that Augustine began to read more about Christianity. His mother had planted seeds of faith in Augustine's heart and mind when he was growing up, and although he ran from his faith for a time, his conscience continued to remind him of who he was and who God was. Augustine would say in his *Confessions*, "Give me chastity . . . only not yet." He knew what he wanted and needed, yet he allowed the flesh and sin to take over.

I've been where Augustine was. There was a point in my life when I knew I wasn't happy or fulfilled. I would begin to make changes, but then I'd go back to my old ways. Like Augustine, I struggled to cut ties with the comforts of a sinful life—its false freedoms and pleasures that left me empty. Yet God never stopped loving me. Nor did he stop loving Augustine.

God doesn't sit back! He is always pursuing us, gently and lovingly, as a devoted Father who longs to be in a relationship with us. Augustine ran from God and God pursued him, just as he pursues you and me.

During his time of searching and longing, as Augustine began to open his heart to God's grace, his father died. Perhaps because of Monica's fervent prayers for her husband, Patricius experienced a conversion on his deathbed and turned his life over to God. Patricius, too, had been running from God and finally stopped, allowing himself to rest in the Father's love. Patricius's conversion did not go unnoticed by Augustine.

The role a father plays in his kids' lives is crucial. If you are a dad, you know this. Read any statistics about the mental, physical, and spiritual health of kids, and you will notice that the engagement of the father is a key factor. Interestingly, the one common denominator when it comes to children living their faith as adults is the example of their father.

My friend's dad was a successful businessman, yet he struggled with addictions to sex, drinking, and gambling. My friend followed in his father's footsteps, experiencing financial success but struggling with addiction. He eventually entered rehab, counseling, and AA and found a faith-based community that helped him change his generational path. The fruit of his hard work can be seen in his loving wife and children.

As the father goes, so goes the family. That's a ton of pressure on us men, pressure we'd rather not have. So, like Augustine, we spend our time becoming gritty but not holy. The great news is that in the Christian life the pressures we experience can be overcome by grace, God's presence living in us. We don't have to be perfect men, husbands, or fathers. We just have to say yes to God, stop running, and allow God to catch up to us. We can model our lives after God the Father. Jesus teaches us how. I believe that Augustine ran from God largely because his father had modeled that behavior for him. God's grace, however, was more than sufficient for both of them to change.

Monica continued to speak truth into her son's life. Her faithful witness of God's love was the most consistent thing he had. She loved her son, even in his worst moments, as God loves us, his sons. Monica, whom we know today as St. Monica, played a major role in Augustine's conversion. She is the ideal saint to pray to for our children who might be far from God.

Augustine relates the story of his conversion in his *Confessions*. He and his friend Alypius were out in the garden one day in Milan when Augustine heard the voice of a child in the neighboring house. The child was chanting over and over again, "Pick it up, read it. Pick it up, read it." Augustine, who had been feeling great inner turmoil, sensed that this chant was a divine command to open and read the scriptures. He picked up his Bible from the bench where he had left it and read the first passage his eyes fell upon. It was from Paul's letter to the Romans: "Not in orgies and drunkenness, not in promiscuity and licentiousness, not in rivalry and jealousy.

But put on the Lord Jesus Christ, and make no provision for the desires of the flesh" (13:13–14).

Augustine felt the light of faith infuse his heart as he read these words. He turned totally from his life of sin and was baptized in the year 387, along with his friend Alypius and his son Adeodatus.

I can relate to Augustine. I know what it's like to run from God. I know what it's like to pursue things other than God, things that are temporary. I finally made the decision to walk away from my old ways. Through lots of prayer, and God's mercy and forgiveness, I did. Through the help of the Church, the sacraments, and good friends, I began to experience real change.

The reality is that we are moved more by Augustine's conversion and his changed ways than by his past. We need and want that change as well. Augustine was a man of grit who eventually gave his heart to God and became a man of holy grit—a man we know centuries later as St. Augustine, one of the fathers of the Church.

THE FOUR B'S

Years ago, I was invited to speak at a men's conference. The organizer of the conference asked me to come up with a talk based specifically on the theme of obstacles faced by men in pursuit of Christ. Not long after I began planning and studying for this speech, I worked at a sports camp where a former coach who was a strong Christian gave a motivational talk. He spoke with conviction, not holding back punches. The men listened, and so did I! I can't remember all of what he said, but I recall that he laid out his message with a few words beginning with the letter B. That got me thinking about what I will call the four B's: the ballfield, the billfold, the bedroom, and the boardroom (thanks, Coach). These four B's present

obstacles that can get in the way of our relationship with
Christ.

The Ballfield

Whether or not you grew up playing a sport, the ballfield represents man's desire to compete. We are wired to fight battles.
Many of us start out competing on little-league fields, trying
to beat the other four-year-olds. We are taught to win, sometimes at all costs. Some of us join a band, pick up a hobby,
invent things—whatever it is, we are looking to be the best, to
beat someone else at our craft. The goal is: I'm the best, and
you are not. I often say women compare, men compete. The
truth is that men do both; we size each other up and compare
ourselves to the other guys in the room. And when we compete with each other, we want to win, no matter what!

The ballfield isn't a bad thing. St. Augustine spent the
better part of his life competing and fighting for truth and
goodness. He stood boldly for the Gospel in a time of great
persecution. When we live in truth, authentically and virtuously, the ballfield is the place where we learn to win at life
and at the same time help others to do the same. However,
when the ballfield is a place of pride, ego, and selfishness, we
don't hesitate to knock someone out to gain an advantage.

Our best battles are fought for things that are good and
holy. The ballfield is where we can sanctify competition and
bring dignity to others. It's here that we can compete to put
our wives and kids first. It's here where we strive to put God
at the apex, the center of our hearts. It's here that we learn
to defend the less fortunate, the needy, those whom society
labels less-than.

Jesus asked, "What profit would there be for one to gain
the whole world and forfeit his life?" (Mt 16:26). This is not
a moment to look at someone else, but in the mirror, and

answer the question: What good is it if I gain everything on the ballfield and in the process lose myself—my soul?

The Billfold

Whether you consider yourself rich or poor, the billfold represents man's desire for success, to win at life by the acquisition of money and other material things. Some of us have more than others, but let's be honest: even when we have plenty, it's not enough. The billfold, money, isn't the problem. Money is like food—we need it to live. And like food, we can use it for good or we can abuse it. But the drive to find our identity in making money and having more "stuff" is strong. Men are made to work; it's in our DNA.

The billfold can be used to raise and support our families, to provide food and a roof over our heads. It can be used to help people in need or to give a job to someone who's lost one. I've seen the good that money can do. I've also seen people get trapped in it.

The virtue, the holy thing for us men, is to be detached from money—to use it for good and to share it with others, no matter how much or how little we have. The vice is for us to seek money for itself, find fulfillment in it, and lose ourselves in the search for happiness through it. I distinctly remember talking with a guy who told me, "I've arrived at financial success, and it's not what I thought it would be. I'm not fulfilled." He expressed his regret and described how his pursuit of "arriving" cost his marriage and his relationship with his children. Now in his sixties, he's spending his time repairing what he broke along the way to success.

Jesus minced no words when he said, "It is easier for a camel to pass through the eye of a needle than for one who is rich to enter the kingdom of God" (Mt 19:24). Those are tough words to swallow, but Jesus speaks them for our own good, for our freedom. Being owned by something is not freedom. The weight of wealth is not ours to carry, but his. Money is given to us to use for good, to bring glory and honor to him. The challenge for us is to allow our hearts to be detached from the billfold and attached to his will.

The Bedroom

The bedroom symbolizes man's sexuality and the lure to find his identity in sex. From an early age, boys are given mixed messages about the meaning of sex and the attraction of lust.

Man's desire to give himself, to sacrifice and be heroic, is built into his heart. Yet the lure of lust and the temptation to prove oneself by using others, especially women, can make us lose our way, maybe never to return. Many men are burdened by the weight of shame, trapped in the bondage of sexual sin.

Just ask St. Augustine. What was toughest for him to walk away from was not the life of success, but the life of lust. Augustine wanted to love and be loved, yet all the while he used others and even himself to find fulfillment. For many years he was trapped in this lifestyle, far away from true happiness. I too got lost here as a young adult, and I have spent years helping men see a new vision for their life and their sexuality. Unfortunately, I've seen men weighed down by shame and regret, having lost what they loved the most by getting trapped in the lures of the bedroom.

Some men forgo getting married because of sexual sin and addiction. Men leave their marriages because of it too. Finding pleasure in the bedroom is the way some men try to fulfill a deep longing. Yet our hearts are only fulfilled when we open them to God and allow him to breathe new life into them.

God created men—you, me, Augustine—to be a gift to another. Man is built to give of himself, to offer his life, as a sacrifice for others. When a man gives his heart and his body to his spouse, this is pleasing to God. This is true freedom. In a sacramental marriage, a man gives not out of lust but out of self-offering, putting his wife, his lover, first and creating life as a fruit of that gift. A priest, too, gives his whole self to the Church, his bride, as a pleasing offering to God the Father. Jesus did the same when he freely offered his life for you and me.

Jesus said, "Everyone who looks at a woman with lust has already committed adultery with her in his heart" (Mt 5:28). These are tough words, but words Jesus speaks to keep you and me from being trapped in the bondage of our own lustful desires. Instead, with God's grace, we can be heroic in how we love.

The Boardroom

The boardroom represents man's hunger for power, fame, and popularity. It also represents a deep desire to be known, loved, and respected—for someone to look across the table and notice us. Will anyone—my boss, my coworkers, my children, my wife—notice me? We long, even as adults, for our parents to notice us, for our dad to look at us and tell us he's proud of our accomplishments. We grew up saying "Watch this" to our parents, and when we weren't seen, we felt alone. That loneliness pushes us to seek affirmation anywhere we can. Of the four B's, the boardroom means . . . I will get noticed no matter what!

I once worked for a boss who was feared by everyone, including me. All of us walked on eggshells, hoping to please him and to avoid his rage. He had power, and he used it to bolster his ego. You could see the loneliness and isolation in his eyes. He longed for more than power could give. He wanted a real connection and tried to find it by buying relationships.

We all long to be rewarded, noticed, praised. The boardroom can be a war room or a safe haven. It can be a place where dreams come true or where people get shredded. Man's ego, his pride, his grasp for power becomes magnified in the

boardroom when the ladder to success requires stepping on
the backs of others. Conversely, the boardroom can be a place
where people are encouraged and empowered. As we grow
in holy grit, we become models of Christ in the boardroom,
serving, empowering, and helping other people become the
best versions of themselves.

Jesus said, "The greatest among you must be your servant.
Whoever exalts himself will be humbled; but whoever hum-
bles himself will be exalted" (Mt 23:11–12). We find true freedom not in lording it over others but in serving them, seeing
ourselves and the face of Christ in the person sitting across
the boardroom table.

AN INVITATION

Our past or present doesn't define who we are, for we are much
more than our mistakes and achievements. We are more than
what we do in our careers, or what we've done (good or bad)
in the past. We are God's sons.

We all have a story, a history, a past. Our upbringing and
family life play an essential role in the direction our life takes,
and none of us have perfect upbringings or families. Like St.
Augustine, we live with the hand we are dealt, until we can't
live that way any longer. My life certainly came to that point—
the point where I wanted more and I needed to change.

I remember finding a Bible in my time of desperation, and
for the first time in my life I opened it and began to read it.
The Word of God became alive to me, as it did for Augustine, and my heart began to well up. I read about a God who
sent his son, Jesus, to save me. And in that moment, I knew I
needed God more than I needed my next breath. I knelt down
on the side of my bed and prayed that God would save me,
would come to my rescue. This was only the beginning for
me, but it was an important first step.

Conversion, as we saw with Augustine, is a process. It happens over time. Some men have dramatic turning points, involving an immediate change of heart. But those moments are just the beginning of the process. And for most of us, conversion results from a bunch of little grace-filled moments that we don't always recognize. These move us forward.

In my book *Rethink Happiness,* I talk about conversion in more detail. The word "conversion" in Greek means "to rethink"—to look at things through new lenses, to begin to understand things as God does. Conversion is a process of both the heart and the mind, where God, with his mighty hands, brings those two aspects of our nature together. This takes time. As Augustine's conversion deepened, he realized with his mind that chastity would bring him true freedom, but his heart had yet to align with his thinking. Thus his famous prayer, "Give me chastity . . . only not yet."

My immediate conversion as a young man was only the first step, the step where I gave my life to Christ and I began to change. But conversion is a daily journey. My actions needed to change, and that takes time. My thoughts needed to change, and that takes time. My understanding needed to change, and that takes time. I am still walking the path of conversion, and will be doing so all of my life.

The good news is that God journeys with us. He pursues us, giving us the grace we need. I, like St. Augustine, had a conversion through sacred scripture. I began to read the Word of God, and it became alive to me. It provided the answers I needed, the path I desired, and the person of Jesus to fall in love with.

St. Augustine wrote, "To fall in love with God is the greatest romance; to seek him the greatest adventure; to find him, the greatest human achievement." Let this be the invitation for us moving forward.

ACTION PLAN

1. Take some time to journal about the obstacles you face on the ballfield, with the billfold, in the bedroom, or in the boardroom. Where is God inviting you to change in one of these areas?

2. Pray this week for the intercession of St. Augustine for specific areas of conversion you desire to embrace.

3. Block off time on your schedule to go to Confession. Then do it.

Prayer of St. Augustine

Too late have I loved you, O Beauty so ancient, O Beauty so new.

Too late have I loved you! You were within me but I was outside myself, and there I sought you!

In my weakness, I ran after the beauty of the things you have made.

You were with me, and I was not with you.

The things you have made kept me from you—the things which would have no being unless they existed in you!

You have called, you have cried, and you have pierced my deafness.

You have radiated forth, you have shined out brightly, and you have dispelled my blindness.

You have sent forth your fragrance, and I have breathed it in, and I long for you.

I have tasted you, and I hunger and thirst for you.

You have touched me, and I ardently desire your peace.

DISCUSSION/JOURNALING QUESTIONS

1. What stands out to you about the life of St. Augustine? How can you relate to him?

2. Which of the four B's resonate with you the most and why?

3. Where or how is God inviting you to change in your life?

4. Reflect on the passage from Romans that was so influential for Augustine: "Not in orgies and drunkenness, not in promiscuity and licentiousness, not in rivalry and jealousy. But put on the Lord Jesus Christ, and make no provision for the desires of the flesh" (13:13–14). How does this challenge you?

3

WE HAVE A JOB

Fighting our spiritual battles with St. Thomas More

Thomas More considered joining a religious order as a young man, but he desired marriage and a family. So this is the vocation he chose. We don't often hear about saints who were married, but there were many. Some of us reading this book are either married or considering marriage as our vocation, and Thomas More is one of those saints we can look to as a life model.

Thomas was happily married with four children when his wife, Jane, died unexpectedly during childbirth. Thomas relied heavily on his faith as he fought to stay on his feet and keep his young family intact. At one point he made a profound statement: "What is deferred is not avoided." He meant that whatever battles of life are in front of us won't go away when we put them aside. We must face them head-on, fight, and allow God to move us through them.

I could spend my life unpacking this statement from Thomas. So many of our battles in life have developed into major warfare because of our tendency to brush them off, hoping they will go away. Most of our patterns of negative behavior begin as small fires. When we don't face them and put them out, they begin to spread, and soon we find ourselves overwhelmed by raging flames.

I often meet with couples who say they are not happy in their marriage and are considering divorce. I have great compassion for these folks and what they are going through. My wife and I, both together and individually, have helped some of these couples find happiness and love again. However, we have also seen couples whose marriages fail, for various reasons. I would say that those whose marriages do not survive have one thing in common: their marital issues did not start overnight. The couples usually experienced problems even before the marriage began. As the marriage took shape, small things, unresolved over time, grew into issues that seemed insurmountable. This can happen in other areas of our lives as well—a molehill becomes a mountain, and before we know it, it seems like we can't get over the top to the other side.

Our lives have weeds. Many men I talk to would rather pretend there are no weeds than do the hard work of pulling them out. If they aren't weeds from our past or our mistakes, they are weeds that sprout from wounds. They are weeds that spring from the realities of life. And the enemy, the devil, will also plant weeds in our lives to cause chaos and confusion.

In the Genesis story, the Garden of Eden was weedless; Adam and Eve were free to live as God designed. Yet the devil set a trap and planted weeds to distract them from living the abundant life God had created for them. They soon found themselves hiding in the weeds of shame. That's where we end up too. Hiding in the weeds.

So too were the Israelites, God's people, made for freedom. They were made to live in the Promised Land. Yet they found themselves in Egypt, encamped in the weeds of slavery.

This was not God's design for them. God had a plan to remove the weeds of slavery and set them free. Just as God moved in the Garden of Eden to find and save Adam and Eve, so too would he seek to save the Israelites from bondage.

As he traveled with his people to the Promised Land, God did not move the Red Sea to one side, leaving a clear path for the Israelites to travel on. No, he "split [the sea] in two" (Ex 14:16), with "the water as a wall to their right and to their left" (v. 22). The Israelites, with God's help, had to muster the courage to walk through the sea with massive walls of water rising up on either side of them. Freedom stood on the other side, and all they needed to do was walk forward. Behind them, the battlefield was closing in, as the Pharaoh and his army followed in hot pursuit. The enemy surely tempted God's people to turn around in fear and head back to Egypt, into slavery again. Yet the Israelites followed God's lead and "walked on dry land through the midst of the sea" (v. 29).

Like the Israelites, we have real battles to fight. The enemy comes after all of us, planting weeds in small ways or big. We should be aware that a battle is raging for our hearts and for our freedom to live as God wants us to live.

As a widower, Thomas was faced with uncertainty, yet he embraced God's grace and moved forward. The battle for his family was real, and Thomas chose to walk through the Red Sea in trust. A few years later, Thomas wed another remarkable woman, Alice Middleton. They were married for twenty-four years until Thomas's death at the age of fifty-seven.

An accomplished lawyer, Thomas was elected to Parliament at the age of twenty-six. He was a man of high moral character whom King Henry VIII relied on and trusted. Thomas did not set out to climb the ladder within England's political structure, but it was where God had placed him to serve and to work. So he did his duty with passion, vigor, and conviction—with grit. He even received the elite title of Sir!

Thomas saw his daily life, his work, and his family as the mission to which he was called. Holding ever higher government positions gave him the opportunity to bring the love of God to those places. Never derailed by his title or his power, he consistently stayed the course, allowing his faith, morals, and convictions to determine his decisions. Thomas strived to put God first in all things. Although he worked for the king of England, he fought hard to make sure God alone sat on the throne of his heart. Like you and me, Thomas worked to remove the weeds and allow God to be number one in his life.

I've spent my life working toward putting God first. It's not easy. In fact, it is hard. Sometimes we have to make tough decisions in order to keep God where he belongs. Jesus said that the greatest commandment is to "love the Lord, your God, with all your heart, with all your soul, and with all your mind" (Mt 22:37). God first. God at the center. God as the apex. God on the throne . . . however you want to say it, we are created to love God with our whole being.

Thomas More said, "What does it avail to know that there is a God, which you not only believe by faith, but also know by reason: what does it avail that you know Him if you think little of Him?" These words challenge us to ask ourselves some honest questions. Is God number one in my life? Am I fighting the battle with him each and every day?

We all have distractions in our life. Many of these distractions keep us from seeing clearly. The enemy will do whatever he can to keep us from allowing God to be the center of our life. St. Paul urged us to "keep our eyes on the prize" (see Philippians 3:14)—that is, to stay focused on Jesus and not get pulled into the weeds, the traps of the enemy.

Life in the early 1500s was difficult. Nothing came easy for Thomas. He fought many battles both politically and personally. But his ultimate downfall was actually his ultimate success. Thomas challenged the king's beliefs about Church doctrine and teaching. King Henry VIII believed his authority gave him the right to change Church teaching as well as to lead the Church of England. Demonstrating holy grit, Thomas refused to acknowledge the king as the head of the Catholic Church. Thomas was a friend of the king and his close counselor, but he served God first and would not back down in the face of extreme political and personal pressure.

In June of 1535, More was indicted and formally tried for the crime of treason, defiance to the king. As a lawyer, More defended himself at his trial, refusing to answer many questions in order not to incriminate himself. He was nevertheless sentenced to death. After the verdict, he finally spoke out in open opposition to what he had previously defied through silence and refusal. God first!

On July 6, 1535, More came before the executioner to be beheaded. "I die the king's good servant," he told those present, "but God's first." His head was displayed on London Bridge as a scare tactic for those who thought about denying the king's authority. His head was later returned to his daughter Margaret, who preserved it as a holy relic of her father. Pope Leo XIII beatified More in 1886, and he was canonized by Pope Pius XI on May 19, 1935. His title would no longer be Sir Thomas More, but St. Thomas More, a champion and model for us to follow.

A BATTLE TO FIGHT

In the last chapter, I talked about the four B's: the ballfield, the billfold, the bedroom, and the boardroom. You could say the fifth B is the battlefield. The battlefield can be described as the place where we live each day, fighting to live the life God designed for us. It is also the place where the rubber meets the road, where real temptations happen in our life.

I wish I could say that the battlefield is simply a meta-phor, but let's face it, the battles we fight each day are real. And we don't even see many of the spiritual battles we face. St. Thomas More, who fought many spiritual battles, said, "We cannot go to heaven in feather beds." We lose the spiritual battles if we take the easy road, but we win them when we face them head-on with God. They aren't easy to fight, but these battles are worth it. Thomas died with no regrets about how he lived his life and what he stood for.

Many years ago, I read a book called *Wild at Heart*, by Christian author and speaker John Eldredge. Eldredge poses a scenario in which every man has a battle to fight. The battle has two distinct aspects.

First is the battle for man's heart, our heart, and who will reign over it. St. Thomas More fought this battle when he was challenged to deny his faith before the king. He also faced the temptation to place power, money, and popularity before his family. Many things vied for the throne of Thomas's heart, but he fought to the end to keep God as his King and Lord.

As each man fights to protect his own heart, he comes alive and finds a purpose. This is the second part of the battle. He fights for the hearts of others, particularly those of his wife and children. This is his vocation. This is his flock. St. Thomas More is a model for fighting for one's family. He was a good husband and father, faithful and true to the end. He placed his family first, even as he rose in popularity and prestige.

Thomas's life and Eldredge's book both paint a picture of what we experience in life, a battle that we often don't see: a spiritual battle. The spiritual battle is not something we talk about or even hear about much from the pulpit, but it is real. We like to be comfortable and be told things will be easy. We prefer homilies that don't challenge us too much. But I can't pretend, and I can't read the gospels with rose-colored lenses. I believe that men want to know the truth and to live in the reality of what's at stake. The spiritual battle is real, and we have a role to play in it!

Scripture says, "Be sober and vigilant. Your opponent the devil is prowling around like a roaring lion looking for [someone] to devour" (1 Pt 5:8). Who and what does the devil want to devour? Us. Our freedom. Our opportunity to become our true selves, to live the life God wants for us. In one of the most loved passages of the Bible, Jesus says, "I came so that they might have life and have it more abundantly"(Jn 10:10). Jesus offers us a life of true freedom and purpose. All of us desire to live abundantly. We all want to live in freedom. This is how Thomas More lived—free and indifferent to the world.

In the same verse, however, Jesus warns us, "The thief comes only to steal and slaughter and destroy" (Jn 10:10). Those are direct words about the enemy's intention to rob us of the abundant life God offers us. When I look at my own journey, I can see the areas where the enemy tempts me, lies to me, and takes my vision and attention away from what is good. If we go back to the four B's, we can evaluate the cracks in our armor and know where our weaknesses are. We don't fight these battles alone. We have Jesus, the true Ruler, King, and Lord. He is our Savior. He has won the victory and claimed our freedom, so we aren't called to fight alone.

Jesus began his public ministry in the desert, where he fought a spiritual battle with the devil. There he was faced with temptation. The devil tempted Jesus three times: to give in to the desires of the flesh (hunger), to put God's providential care to the test, and to take claim over worldly power and possessions (see Matthew 4:1–11). Prior to Jesus entering the desert for forty days, he was baptized. It is fitting that Jesus's identity as the Son of God was affirmed before he left to face the devil. The Gospel of Mark describes this event: "On coming up out of the water he saw the heavens being torn open and the Spirit, like a dove, descending upon him. And a voice came from the heavens, 'You are my beloved Son; with you I am well pleased'" (1:10–11). God spoke, the Holy Spirit was present, and the Son received loving recognition of his sacred identity. Jesus modeled for us what happens at our baptism, where God claims us as his sons and affirms our true call and purpose.

The Holy Spirit is present at our baptism. He claims our hearts, sets an indelible mark on our souls, and comes to live in us. The authority of Jesus, Lord and King, is placed on the throne of our hearts, where it reigns victoriously so that we can live fully.

Jesus battled openly with the devil in the desert. He battled against evil throughout his earthly journey, in the Garden of Gethsemane, and during his Passion. He not only claimed victory over the enemy's power but taught us that through prayer and fasting we can, with his grace, fight off the enemy and be victorious each day.

AN INVITATION

I grew up fishing frequently. It was one of the things that my dad and I did together, and it was good. When we fished for largemouth bass, we used artificial baits called lures. What I eventually realized is that a lure is simply something that is disguised as something else. The rubber worm is meant to look like a real worm, and the plastic fish is meant to look like a real minnow. Embedded in these lures is a hook that the fish doesn't know about. Thus we have a fake bait with a real hook to attract the fish into biting. And it works.

This is how the enemy works in our life. He is a master fisherman. He lures us into biting something that we think is good, yet there is a hidden hook. Simply put, the devil takes what is good, what is true, and twists it into a lie. When I'm fishing, I'm lying to the fish, tempting it to bite something that looks real but is not. So too, the devil lies to us, just as he lied to Adam and Eve and just as he lied to Jesus in the desert. The devil takes God's goodness and truth and twists it into a lie to tempt us into taking a bite of the hook—the apple.

King Henry VIII offered to spare Thomas More's life if he denied the fullness of the truth. The king presented Thomas with a watered-down truth, a diluted form of the faith with some elements of truth. It was a subtle tactic, and to many, it wouldn't have mattered if Thomas denied his faith to save his life. Yet Thomas was a devout disciple, a prayerful man who leaned heavily on the sacraments and the Holy Spirit to guide him. When friends criticized him for receiving the sacraments frequently, he responded:

> Your reasons for wanting me to stay away from Holy Communion are exactly the ones which cause me to go so often. My distractions are great, but it is in Communion that I recollect myself. I have temptations many times a day; by daily Communion I get the strength to overcome them. I have much very important business to handle and I need light and wisdom; it is for this reason that I go to Holy Communion every day to consult Jesus about them.

Through his deep devotion to prayer, fasting, and the sacraments, Thomas was able to see the hooks hidden in the lures. And although he was tempted, he didn't bite.

Welcome to the battlefield, where the first part of fighting is actually knowing there is a battle going on. Jesus tells us there's a battle, and so does St. Thomas More. They also tell us that we are created to fight this battle, to win, and to thrive. When we know we are made for the battlefield, our hearts come alive. So many men want adventure in their life. Let's skydive. Let's hike, hunt, or fish. These are all good things, as long as we keep them in balance. Or let's drive fast cars, drink too much, gamble, overspend, chase women, live without barriers. Crash and burn.

The desire to do battle runs deep in a man's heart. This is why many young men spend endless hours playing video games; all the while there is some beautiful young lady out there looking for a good man, while he's lost online. Young men today forgo dating, even marriage, because the enemy has enticed them to do something else. Men are created for so much more—a battle to fight and a beauty to find.

The second part of fighting the battle is showing up. I remember the day I got married—I had been stressing nonstop about how to have a good marriage. My friend and mentor told me on the day of the wedding, "Just show up." Showing up was the first step, and if I did that every day, God would take care of the rest. Great advice. God fights alongside us each and every day, but we need to show up for the battle and let God carry us the rest of the way.

As I wrote this chapter, a framed quote from Theodore Roosevelt captured my attention:

> It is not the critic who counts: not the man who points out how the strong man stumbles or where the doer of deeds could have done better. The credit belongs to the man who is actually in the arena, whose face is marred by dust and sweat and blood, who strives valiantly, who errs and comes up short again and again, because there is no effort without error or shortcoming, but who knows the great enthusiasms, the great devotions, who spends himself in a worthy cause; who, at the best, knows, in the end, the triumph of high achievement, and who, at the worst, if he fails, at least he fails while daring greatly, so that his place

shall never be with those cold and timid souls who
knew neither victory nor defeat.

I find that men who are most fulfilled and happy are living for Christ. They are men who are in the arena fighting for something good, "marred by dust" on the spiritual battlefield. These men are alive. They aren't perfect. They have sinned and been forgiven. They are not afraid to walk into the confessional to ask for freedom from their mistakes. They have failed in battle yet have gotten up, linked arms with other brothers in armor, and continued to fight the good fight in a world in need.

These men can say with St. Paul in his writing to St. Timothy, "I have competed well; I have finished the race; I have kept the faith" (2 Tm 4:7). Their battle scars have meaning, and their lives have a purpose. These men, saints of today like those of the past, fight for their hearts, their wives, their children, their flock, their neighbors, and their faith.

The invitation for you and me is to recognize that there is a battle to fight, to show up each day, and to lean on God to do the heavy lifting. Most of all, we are invited to allow Jesus to sit on the throne of our hearts and our lives.

ACTION PLAN

1. St. Thomas More said, "The ordinary acts we practice every day at home are of more importance to the soul than their simplicity might suggest." Do something this week to place your family first. Take your wife on a date. Spend time with your children. If you are a priest, visit a family in need. If you are single, reach out to a friend you haven't spoken with in a while or visit an older family member.

2. Firm up your battlefield defense. Make a list of things you can do and people you can rely on to help you fight the good fight each day.

3. St. Thomas More went to Mass often, more than just on Sunday. Make time to attend Mass once or twice during the week.

Prayers of St. Thomas More

FOR RESISTANCE TO TEMPTATION

Almighty God, who of your infinite goodness did create our first parents in the state of innocence, with present wealth and hope of heaven to come till through the devil's deceit their folly fell by sin to wretchedness: by your tender pity of that Passion that was paid for their and our redemption, assist me with your gracious help so that to the subtle suggestions of the serpent I never so incline the ears of my heart but that my reason may resist them and master my sensuality and keep me from them.

FOR FERVENT LOVE OF CHRIST

O my sweet Savior Christ, who in your undeserved love towards mankind so kindly would suffer the painful death of the cross: suffer not me to be cold or lukewarm in love again towards you.

DISCUSSION/JOURNALING QUESTIONS

1. St. Thomas More is quoted as saying, "Give me the grace, good Lord . . . to know my own vileness and wretchedness. To humble myself under the mighty hand of God. To bewail my sins and, for the purging of them, patiently to suffer adversity." How have you been lured by the enemy lately? Have you been engaged in the spiritual battle of life? Take some time to reflect on the subtle ways the enemy seeks to distract you.

2. St. Thomas More is also quoted as saying, "Grant me, O Lord, a sense of good humor. Allow me the grace to be able to take a joke, to discover in life a bit of joy, and to be able to share it with others." Do you take life too seriously at times? Have you allowed yourself to experience joy lately? What things in life steal your joy? How can you share the joy of Christ with others and yourself?

3. Reflect on God sitting on the throne of your life, your heart. What are the things that vie for that seat? How can you allow Jesus to be number one in your life daily?

4

OUR TRUE IDENTITY

Embracing who we are with St. Ignatius of Loyola

The life of St. Ignatius of Loyola can be summed up as a tale of two halves. During the first half of his life, he searched for meaning and purpose. He also sought success and prestige. Later he admitted that this half of his life was far from God—successful yet empty, comfortable yet hollow. Ignatius lived the second half of his life with Christ by his side and in his heart, wholeheartedly learning to love God, himself, and others as Christ does. Ignatius lived both halves of his life with passion and grit.

I can relate to Ignatius. I also spent the first part of my life with no boundaries, in search of meaning, only thinking of myself and my own path forward. I was outwardly thriving and inwardly desperate. I was winning, yet losing.

I played sports through college, but let's face it, the glory days were really in high school. I remember one game when we were winning by a lot at halftime. We weren't playing well but our opponent was inferior, so we were confident. At halftime we gathered in the locker room with high fives, laughter, and lots of fun. Our coach walked in, picked up a large trashcan, and threw it across the room. It hit the wall with a loud crash. Coach proceeded to berate us for the way we were playing. We were winning; the scoreboard said so. But, although we might be winning over the opponent, we were losing in our potential as a team. We took Coach's words to heart. During the second half, we didn't play against our opponent but against ourselves, and we played lights out. We gave it our all.

I find that many men, myself included, live the way our team was playing in the first half—minimally. We may act as though life is great. We may believe we are winning, but the truth is that we aren't living to our full potential. What if our lives, like Ignatius's, became a tale of two halves? And in the second half we lived life to the full, the way we were created to live?

Luckily for Ignatius, he survived the first half of his life, the time when he was far from God. Many men aren't so fortunate; they make choices that result in spiritual or even physical death. If you are reading this book, it's not too late!

Ignatius was born on October 23, 1491, in Azpeitia, Spain, to a fairly wealthy family. As a young man he was mentored to become successful, eventually earning the title of knight. Ignatius was soon trusted with diplomatic affairs and military operations. He became a warrior and a leader on the battlefield.

During one battle Ignatius was struck by a cannonball and then confined to the infirmary. His injury was serious and brought him close to death. Lying in bed for long periods of time, Ignatius began to read. The only reading material available was the Bible and books about the lives of the saints. It was there, in bed, weak and vulnerable, that Ignatius's heart began to break. The very thing he had been searching for, God, was close to him in his darkest hours. Ignatius's conversion began with a war wound in an infirmary he never thought he'd leave.

I have already mentioned that "conversion" in Greek means to "rethink." Conversion involves thinking about our lives and our purpose in a new way. As we seek, ask, and think, our minds and hearts are moved and transformed. They turn away from the old and toward the new. We turn away from sin and toward God, a new life in Christ. St. Ignatius said, "Sin is unwillingness to trust that what God wants for me is only my deepest happiness."

Like Ignatius, I was struggling with a wound at the time of my conversion, though mine was spiritual rather than physical. I was lying in bed, wounded by life and by my sin, when I began to read scripture. I was hoping to find something that the world couldn't offer, and I did. I read in the letter to the Romans, "If you confess with your mouth that Jesus is Lord and believe in your heart that God raised him from the dead, you will be saved" (10:9). Upon reading this, I knelt down at the side of my bed and invited the God of the universe, Jesus, to save me, and he did.

As a result of his conversion, Ignatius finally discovered who he was: God's beloved son. This is what we all desire to find—our true identity as God's cherished children. Discovering his sonship in Christ catapulted Ignatius to leave his old life and begin anew.

In his *Spiritual Exercises*, Ignatius shares some of the insights he received about our purpose and identity as God's children:

> God freely created us so that we might know, love, and serve him in this life and be happy with him forever. God's purpose in creating us is to draw forth from us a response of love and service here

on earth, so that we may attain our goal of everlasting happiness with him in heaven.

All the things in this world are gifts of God,
created for us, to be the means by which we can
come to know him better, love him more surely,
and serve him more faithfully.

As a result, we ought to appreciate and use
these gifts of God insofar as they help us toward
our goal of loving service and union with God.
But insofar as any created things hinder our progress toward our goal, we ought to let them go.

After Ignatius recovered from his injury, he began his new
journey as a convert to Christ, eventually entering seminary
and being ordained to the priesthood. What makes Ignatius
a man among men is that he gave his all in everything. This
is what men desire and what men are created for: to live fully.
Ignatius has had a tremendous impact on the world, and it's
all from the "second half"!

I often encounter men who have settled for who they are
and given up on the possibility of significant change. As for
me, I sit here in my middle age and wonder about where my
journey with Christ will lead me next. The "second half" of
our life doesn't begin at a certain age; it's a new chapter that
begins when we encounter Christ and rethink our lives in light
of our relationship with him. The process of conversion can
begin at any time. Sometimes we think it's too late for change
and feel paralyzed by shame we carry from our past. Maybe
we drag our feet because of a lack of courage or fear of failure.
Maybe it's a lack of conviction and purpose. With great wisdom, Ignatius said, "When taking the first steps on the road
of virtue the old man must be mortified, but in such a way as
not to slay the new man." We can't worry about what's next,

but trust that God will lead us. Ignatius continued, "Undertake nothing without consulting God."

Pope Paul III gave Ignatius permission to found the Society of Jesus, a religious order more commonly known as the Jesuits, in 1540. This movement sent missionaries worldwide, bringing the Gospel to people who had never heard the name of Jesus. Many Jesuit missionaries worked in dangerous regions, losing their lives to martyrdom for the sake of Christ. They were men with holy grit. Almost five hundred years later, the Jesuits continue to serve around the world.

Ignatius spent the last days of his life sick and infirm, lying in bed as in the early days of his conversion. There he prayed and eventually met Jesus face-to-face, dying in 1556. Ignatius was canonized by Pope Gregory XV in 1622, leaving behind the title of knight and earning the new title of St. Ignatius of Loyola.

EMBRACING WHO WE ARE

Who am I? As men, we often find our identity in what we do for a living or what we are good at. Our work. Our hobbies. Our buddies. Our humor. Our reputation. Our grit. Our values. Our politics. This is who I am.

As men, we also connect our identity with things we feel inadequate in. We often avoid those things because we don't like to experience feelings of inadequacy. So we connect "who I am" with "what I'm not." I'm not good at labor. Or building things. Or making money. Or fixing cars. Or sports. Or school. Or relationships. Or making my wife happy. Or talking with my children. And so on.

We men tend to stay close to the things we do well, because venturing into the unknown, especially emotionally and spiritually, is terrifying. We'd rather stay in a box where we know we are competent than try something new and fail. Being competent allows us to feel manly, like we have what it takes to accomplish the task at hand. Feeling adequate is important to us. I'm not talking here about our natural gifts and the ability to work in our areas of expertise and strengths. Staying in our lane in these areas certainly makes sense. But I'm talking here about living according to our true identity, not having to prove anything to anyone, particularly God.

When thinking about who they are, men tend to volley between "what I do" and "what I can't/don't do," trying to keep the ball in the court emotionally, spiritually, and physically. We find it difficult to accept that "who I am" has nothing to do with "what I do" or "what I can't/don't do." Often we don't stop long enough to ponder this question of identity that is deep in our souls until, like St. Ignatius, we get hit by a cannonball.

Let's go back to the baptism of Jesus in the Jordan River. He had not even begun his public ministry at this point. By the world's standards he had accomplished nothing. Yet as Jesus came up from the water, God the Father said, "This is my beloved Son, with whom I am well pleased" (Mt 3:17). Why did God speak these specific words? God only speaks truth and only speaks with purpose. God delivered these words for a reason. First, he spoke directly to his Son about the truth of who he was: God's beloved. These words of God have power. Being confirmed in his identity strengthened Jesus to go into the desert to fight and win. Second, God spoke those words to us as well. When Jesus was baptized, he modeled for us what we are called to do. He instituted the Sacrament of Baptism, allowing us to join with him and have new life. Those same words that were spoken powerfully over Jesus are now spoken over us in our baptism. Those words, "my beloved Son, with whom I am well pleased," are meant for you and me.

St. Ignatius wrestled with his identity for the first part of his life, finding his worth in what he accomplished. It wasn't until he was wounded by war and couldn't do anything that he began to realize his true identity, his sonship. Who he was, was far greater than what he had accomplished on the battle-field. The grace from his baptism began to well up, stirring in him a newfound friendship with Christ.

Who we are is who we are . . . it's not what we do! This is difficult to accept. I've wrestled with this. Who am I when I'm struggling with work? Who am I when I can't play a sport anymore? Who am I when I fail at home? If who I am is based on my successes and failures, I'm doomed. Why? Because, like you, I am imperfect. I have good days and bad. I live in an emotional battlefield of highs and lows, and if my life is defined by accomplishments, then its value is ever changing. Truth be told, the biggest battle I have faced daily in my life is accepting the truth of my identity as God's beloved son.

We all get cannonballs launched at us, attacking the very thing that God wants us to know about ourselves. This was the same cannonball attack that Satan launched at Jesus in the desert. He begins two of his temptations by questioning Jesus's identity: "If you are the Son of God, command that these stones become loaves of bread. . . . If you are the Son of God, throw yourself down [from the parapet]" (Mt 4:1:3, 6). In man's case, the devil causes us to question and forget the unique status we receive at baptism as God's children. The onslaught he seeks to launch on every man's heart is an attack on his true identity as God's beloved son.

St. Ignatius said, "When the devil wants to attack anyone, he first of all looks to see on what side his defenses are weak-est or in worst order; then he moves up his artillery to make a breach at that spot." I'm convinced that if a man struggles with his identity and simply volleys between "what I do" and "what I can't/don't do" as the foundation of who he is, the enemy will breach the walls of his heart and convince him that he's only loved, he's only accepted, if he can do something.

The words of God the Father at Jesus's baptism tell us a lot about our relationship with him. When God says "my," he indicates that we belong to him. When he says "beloved," he tells us that his love for us is abundant, unending, infinite. When he says "son," he claims us as his own and gives us a divine affiliation; we are God's child. And when God says "with whom I am well pleased," he tells us that his love, his pleasure in us, is unconditional. God's love has nothing to do with what we can accomplish. No, God's love is unconditional and infinite, no matter what!

For St. Ignatius, it was this truth about his identity as God's beloved son that gave him the grace to live the second half of his life as a man with holy grit.

AN INVITATION

I grew up with my feet in a pair of cleats, obsessed from an early age with playing sports. I was good at it, and I also loved it. That was where I found competency in a skill, as well as a safe haven from life's worries. We all know what it's like to find the safe place where we feel competent. For me, playing sports was so interwoven into who I was and what I did that I didn't even know it. You may be able to relate as you think of the many things you do or are good at as part of who you are, such as work, hobbies, and friendships.

When I was on the field, life was manageable. My worries seemed to go away when I was between the lines. I could deal with highs and lows, successes and failures. We men find comfort in living "between the lines," whether that's in work or play; it's the place where we feel adequate and up for the task. But off the field, outside the lines, we often don't have the same confidence, at least I didn't. Off the field I felt like I had no focus, I often felt like a failure, and truthfully, I didn't know who I was. It wasn't until competitive sports ended for me that I was hit with the reality that I didn't fully know myself, my own identity. These were thoughts and feelings that I kept inside. No one knew I felt unworthy or like a failure.

I have numerous conversations with men today who are finally admitting that life is hard. They often say to me, "I feel like I'm not enough" or "I feel like I'm failing at home." These are real concerns that we all experience at times. And it's okay, because God meets us in our weak places, in our inadequacies. God thrives where we don't.

Earlier in my life, when our children were younger, I tried to navigate the constant feeling of incompetency I felt at home and even at work. The answer I gave myself . . . just grit through it. So I worked and traveled more, thinking that the same grind I had on the field would translate to my life now and I could prove to myself and everyone else that I "had what it takes." Men with grit always win, but I was exhausted and could not admit it. My wife wanted me to share more of myself, those parts of my life that seemed emotionally detached, and yet I didn't even know about those parts myself. Working harder seemed to be the solution that everyone else was subscribing to, and my wife and I did too. All the while we are watching each other drown, spiritually and emotionally.

Marriage can be a powerful sacrament of healing, when two imperfect people come together to love each other and commit to one another even in their brokenness. We all carry baggage into our vocation, but it's up to us to open the trunk and take steps to deal with what's in it. My trunk was full and locked. Opening it seemed like a tall task.

To fully know yourself, you must allow God to enter into every crevice of your life and your heart—your trunk. It's difficult to know your identity when you can't see past the things that block your true self. I was challenged by a friend and spiritual counselor to begin to look at the broken and wounded places in my heart. He said it was here, in those places, the cannonball wounds, that I didn't love myself, that I didn't believe God loved me or that I was lovable to others.

Whew! It was a lot to unpack. Yet over time and with much prayer, patience, and spiritual counseling, I began to find God's healing love in the areas of my life where I felt unlovable. I began to love myself, not because of what I could do, but because of who God created me to be. And I began to open my heart to God, others, and especially my wife.

God heals the heart. God heals our wounds, lovingly, as we place the broken pieces of our lives in his care. He also forgives our sins, the very ways our wounds move us to hurt ourselves and others. The loving Father who spoke those powerful words over Jesus at his baptism began to speak those words over me, and I began to live in freedom by accepting those words. I discovered my identity as his beloved son.

Like St. Ignatius, I'm committed to the "second half" of my life being one of holy grit. This is not easy, but men with holy grit always win, because it's God who fights the battle with us and for us. That's the field I want to play on!

St. Ignatius said, "He who carries God in his heart bears heaven with him wherever he goes." This is true. As we allow God to enter our hearts, and allow the Holy Spirit to heal us, we begin to live the life we were created to live.

From the very beginning at our baptism, God claimed us as his own. He proclaimed powerful words over our hearts and gave Jesus authority to reside there. He bestowed the Holy Spirit upon us, giving us the grace to love him, ourselves, and others. Certainly, life throws cannonballs at us, wounding us and distracting us from the reality of who God created us to be. But we aren't defined by our wounds or our incompetence. We are God's beloved sons.

When we allow the grace from our baptism to resurrect us to new life in Christ, we begin anew. Thus, through the power of our baptism and knowing our identity as God's beloved sons, we can do as St. Ignatius said: "Go forth and set the world on fire." We can set our marriages, our churches, and our families on fire. We can set our lives on fire!

ACTION PLAN

1. St. Ignatius said, "Pray as if God will take care of all; act as if all is up to you." Take an inventory of your life. Think about areas that you want and need to grow in. Pray and reflect on those, asking God to give you the grace to take action.

2. Meditate on the words of God at Jesus's baptism: "This is my beloved Son, with whom I am well pleased" (Mt 3:17). How do these words influence your life and how you think about yourself?

3. The enemy seeks to distract and discourage us from living as God's sons. St. Ignatius said, "Discouragement is not from God." Seek out spiritual advice on how to deal with discouragement in your spiritual journey.

Prayers of St. Ignatius

PRAYER OF SURRENDER

Take, O Lord, and receive all my liberty, my memory, my understanding, and my entire will. Whatever I have or hold, you have given me; I restore it all to you and surrender it wholly to be governed by your will. Give me only your love and your grace, and I am rich enough and ask for nothing more.

PRAYER OF SELF-OFFERING

Take, O Lord, and receive my entire liberty, my memory, my understanding, and my whole will. All that I am and all that I possess you have given me: I surrender it all to you to be disposed of according to your will. Give me only your love and your grace; with these I will be rich enough, and will desire nothing more.

DISCUSSION/JOURNALING QUESTIONS

1. In what ways do you struggle with accepting your true identity as God's beloved son?

2. How does the life of St. Ignatius resonate with you? In what ways does his life challenge you to be more holy and gritty?

3. Do you have people in your life who remind you of who you are in Christ?

4. Do you take time in your day to pray and reflect on God's love for you?

5. "I wish not merely to be called Christian, but also to be Christian." What does this quote from St. Ignatius mean to you? How does it call you to be a man of holy grit?

5

A PATH WITH A PURPOSE

Discovering God's plan for us with Padre Pio

The future saint Francesco Forgione was born on May 25, 1887. His parents, Giuseppa and Grazio Forgione, raised their son in a modest, faith-filled environment in the small farming town of Pietrelcina in southern Italy. As a child, Francesco suffered from various illnesses. His family often worried that the boy wouldn't survive, but God had plans for Francesco's life.

Francesco had a heart for God and a strong faith at an early age. He expressed interest in the priesthood and eventually convinced his parents to let him enter religious life at the age of fifteen. He joined the novitiate of the Capuchin friars. His family was so committed to God's unfolding plan for their son that Francesco's father migrated to the United States to find work to pay for academic tutoring before Francesco

entered the seminary. Francesco chose the religious name
Friar Pio when he became a Capuchin.

The *Catechism of the Catholic Church* says, "The desire for
God is written in the human heart, because man is created
by God and for God; and God never ceases to draw man to
himself. Only in God will he find the truth and happiness he
never stops searching for: The dignity of man rests above all
on the fact that he is called to communion with God" (para.
27). We are born with God in our hearts. By nature, our
souls long for union with him. From an early age I knew that
there was something good about me, I knew that there was
something good about other people, and I knew that there
was something good about God. Although it took me a long
time to discover, I finally recognized that God had been in my
heart all along.

By grace, Friar Pio knew that God resided within him.
God lives in your heart, too, from the beginning of your existence. Maybe you are like Friar Pio and you have known this
truth since you were young. Or maybe you are like St. Augustine or St. Ignatius, who realized God's plan later in life.

I remember the moment that someone looked at me and
told me that God had a plan for me. I was a teenager, living
loosely, and a friend invited me to attend a talk at his church.
I was leery about stuff like that—talks about faith and God—
but I went because my friend didn't want to go alone. After the
talk was over and we were driving away, my friend looked at
me and said, "God has a plan for you, you know."

Those eight words made me rethink my life. It was the
first time anyone had ever said that to me, or at least it was
the first time that my heart was receptive to it. It rattled me,
caught my attention, because my heart had been searching
for something more. I was given a path to follow and a plan
to live by: Jesus, who is "the way and the truth and the life"
(Jn 14:6). God has a plan for each one of us. His plan from the

beginning is to be in a relationship with us, in union with his children. We are made for a relationship with God.

I've been told that if you want to make God laugh, you should tell him your plans. This rings true in many ways. God's plans for us are not always our plans for ourselves. And his ways are certainly not our ways, as the prophet Isaiah reminds us: "For my thoughts are not your thoughts, nor are your ways my ways. . . . For as the heavens are higher than the earth, so are my ways higher than your ways, my thoughts higher than your thoughts" (55:8–9).

Although Friar Pio knew that he wanted to live the religious life and become a faithful priest, he did not fully know God's plan for his life. God's plans are better than our own, and his ways have more purpose than ours do. We sometimes prefer to tell God what our plans are and have him agree, rather than ask him to show us his will. Imagine if Friar Pio had told God that he would follow him only under certain conditions. When we make our yes to God conditional on our own terms, we are telling him that we're in charge. But what happens if we totally trust God with our lives, no strings attached?

Many men are afraid to let go of control and allow God to take the reins. This is hard for me as well. Yet our greatest desire is to know God, and his ultimate plan is to unite us with him. God is also in tune with our vocational desires for marriage, priesthood, and other callings. Trusting that he will fulfill our desires is part of surrendering. God knows our gifts and how we can best serve the world. And he wants us to be happy in using our gifts in service of others. Men with grit do what they want and then ask God to bless their plan. But men with holy grit take a different approach. They follow God's plan first, and ask for grace to surrender along the way.

Friar Pio was eventually ordained to the priesthood and took the name Padre (Father) Pio. As a humble Capuchin priest, he received some astonishing spiritual gifts from God: the stigmata, bilocation, healing, prophecy, and the ability to read souls. Receiving and using these gifts in his ministry was never part of his plan for himself, but they were God's plan for him. Part of this plan was for Padre Pio to manifest the actual wounds of Christ, the stigmata. Imagine the suffering that Padre Pio endured when his hands and feet were pierced. Also imagine the grace and the intimacy with Christ that he experienced.

Padre Pio became known throughout the world for his ministry, yet he never desired the attention of others. He remained humble and faithful to God's plan for him, even in the face of popularity and ridicule. Some of the most wonderful stories of Padre Pio describe what happened when he prayed the holy Mass. With his hands wrapped in cloth to keep the wounds of Christ from bleeding down his arms, he would celebrate Mass with a holy passion. Witnesses could feel the power of the Holy Spirit. One parishioner said, "After the consecration his face underwent an amazing change. It seemed to be transfigured with radiant light. From the very first time I went to Mass, I realized that the Spirit of God was there." Many people walked away healed from infirmities after attending Padre Pio's Masses.

When, at an early age, Padre Pio started his journey to follow God, he could never have predicted what God would do. Neither can we. God's plan for us starts with a yes—surrender. Padre Pio said, "Do not worry over things that generate preoccupation, derangement, and anxiety. One thing only is necessary: to lift up your spirit and love God." This is the first step in God's plan for us, to trust and not worry about what's next. Men of holy grit do what Padre Pio did—surrender to Christ and join their hearts to his. This is where God's plans for our lives take root and grow.

Padre Pio remained faithful to God even when people in the Church threw accusations his way. He did not waver in his fidelity to the Church and to the pope. Padre Pio died in 1968 at the age of eighty-one, uniting his wounds with those of the risen Christ. He was canonized in 2002 by Pope John Paul II. We know him today as St. Pio of Pietrelcina.

DISCOVERING GOD'S PLAN

In previous chapters we talked about our identity in Christ and the battle we have to fight, our mission. The power of God's word spoken to us at our baptism remains in our hearts. When we receive the sacraments, such as the Eucharist and Reconciliation, God's grace moves in us. God is active, always extending his love to us.

When I was born, the doctors thought I might not survive because my lungs were undeveloped. Because of the uncertainty my parents had me baptized as an infant in the hospital. As I rose from the waters of baptism, I died with Christ, cleansed from original sin and given new life. At the age of fourteen I was confirmed, not fully knowing what I was doing. There, too, God generously showered grace on me, giving me more of the Holy Spirit to live out my baptismal calling.

Little did I know that through both of these sacraments God's grace was in my soul, moving and healing. God was doing work under the hood of the car, and I had no idea it was happening. I believe that this grace was like a genie trapped in a bottle, waiting to get out. God wanted to move in my life, to renew me. The Holy Spirit was waiting for a crack in the bottle (my heart). I believe that the sacramental grace from those early moments in my life played a massive role in my return to the Lord as a young man. Those graces are active in you, too.

According to the *Catechism*, "Our salvation flows from God's initiative of love for us, because 'he loved us and sent his Son to be the expiation for our sins' (*1 Jn* 4:10). 'God was in Christ reconciling the world to himself' (*2 Cor* 5:19)" (para. 620). One of the great misconceptions of the Christian life is that we do all the work while God sits back as though he's uninterested. Not so! God is active. God is moving. God is the initiator. God is the pursuer, the lover who longs to be united with us.

Our will and ego can move God out of our lives, however. Our hearts can become cold like stone, and we can leave zero space for God. I've heard it said that "ego" stands for "edging God out"—more of me and less of God. Yet God's grace can move through any wall that our heart builds up. As the saying goes, God is never outdone in generosity.

How do we discover God's plan, his path for us each day? St. Pio's first step in discovering God's plan was his next step. St. Pio allowed God's grace to flow in his life one moment, one step, and one day at a time. Why one step at a time? Because if Padre Pio had known what was ahead of him, he might not have said yes to all of it. Not long after his first assignment as a priest, Padre Pio was commissioned to serve in the army. It was a crucial time in World War I. Despite his bad health, Padre Pio took the step to go and serve Jesus in his soldiers on the battlefield. This was never in Padre Pio's plan, yet he found freedom in serving the Lord in whatever way God chose. St. Pio was a man of holy grit! If we want to be men of holy grit, the first step is to allow God to find us. We must take the initiative and surrender our plans to him.

The next step in discovering God's plan is to trust. No one knew this better than St. Pio. He prayed, "My past, O Lord, to Your mercy; my present, to Your love; my future, to Your providence." Trust is hard. It takes practice. And where trust has been broken, healing takes time. When we struggle with trust, there is often a deeper issue at play. How can I trust when someone has hurt me? We project this broken sense of trust onto God, fearing that he will let us down as human beings have.

St. Pio must have had to work hard at trusting God, as the path God chose for him took many different turns. The spiritual gifts God bestowed upon him surely required that he take one step forward at a time, with God leading the way. Besides the stigmata, Padre Pio had the gift of bilocation, the miraculous ability to be in two places at one time. He also had the gift of healing. He prayed for physical, spiritual, and emotional healing for others, and God often granted that healing. Jesus was a healer, and through the Holy Spirit, God wants to continue his healing work even today.

Padre Pio had the gift of prophecy, the ability to speak God's word to help others respond to the call for further conversion. Padre Pio spoke God's truth during a turbulent time in history. He never asked for these gifts, nor did he want them to become public displays.

Many people in the Church, especially those high up in the Vatican, were skeptical of Padre Pio and his spiritual gifts. This was hard for him. As his popularity grew, he was asked not to say Mass publicly. He was investigated. He was questioned. He was humiliated. He was doubted. He was misunderstood. However, through all the mistrust, hurt, suffering, and disappointment he felt, he stayed the course. St. Pio trusted God.

We have all experienced hurt. We have all broken someone's trust in us or had our own trust broken. But this should not discourage us from placing our trust in God. He will never let us down. Proverbs 3:5–6 says, "Trust in the LORD with all your heart, on your own intelligence do not rely; In all your ways be mindful of him and he will make straight your paths." As we surrender our hearts to God's loving care, God heals us and gives us the grace to grow.

God's plan for us is to grow where he plants us. If he needs to uproot us and plant us somewhere else, then so be it. Isaiah says, "See, I am doing something new! Now it springs forth, do you not perceive it? In the wilderness I make a way" (43:19). God makes a way for us. Each step of his plan for us unfolds in his time.

St. Pio became very ill while still a young friar. His superiors sent him to different locations, hoping he would get well. He even went home for a time to stay with his family. Each place he went, Friar Pio blossomed. He loved and served in every location. He wasn't concerned about where he was, but how he was living. One step at a time. Surrender. Trust. Repeat. That was the way of St. Pio.

God's plan will not be easy, and his path will sometimes be narrow. But he will "never fail you or forsake you" (Dt 31:6). St. Pio suffered both physically and spiritually. He often prayed that his stigmata would be healed so that he wouldn't have to bear the physical pain and emotional humiliation any longer. There are things in our own lives that we can't always control, or explain, but God's grace is enough. As God told St. Paul, "My grace is sufficient for you, for power is made perfect in weakness" (2 Cor 12:9).

St. Pio was famously quoted as saying, "Pray, hope, and don't worry. Worry is useless. God is merciful and will hear your prayer." He has shown us the way to seek God with all our heart and to put our trust in him alone. This is a life-long challenge and journey—to grow in trust, to surrender our will, and to take one step at a time. But when we reflect on the life of St. Pio, we see a man of holy grit who has modeled the way for us.

AN INVITATION

What's the next step for us to move forward? Men are build-ers, hunters, and gatherers. Men are fighters, problem solvers, and tinkerers. Men are movers and shakers. Men are inven-tors and implementers. When we use these characteristics for good, God can do amazing things in us. However, when we use them for our self-gratification or for power and ego, they can take us off course.

Imagine what it would be like if we used all that we have, all that we are, to move forward each day with God. St. Pio said, "In the spiritual life he who does not advance goes back-ward. It happens as with a boat which always must go ahead. If it stands still the wind will blow it back." I've spent many days on boats, and I know this to be true about the wind. I've had days where the motor gave out and left me stranded far from land and the wind had its way, taking me even farther from my destination. I needed a tow to make it back.

We all know what it's like to backslide, lose traction. We all know what it's like to break down and need a tow. The truth is that none of us like moving backward, but we need help moving forward. We need God, the Church, and others to tow us.

Men like to make plans to move forward. St. Pio was inten-tional about moving his life forward, even if it was at a snail's pace. God's plan and his pace are where we find freedom, not in our own plan and pace. This is what St. Pio did with his life. You could say that his plan was to live in rhythm with God, always putting prayer first: "Prayer is the best weapon we possess, the key that opens the heart of God." But how do we know God's plan and pace for us?

Years ago, my friend underwent a medical procedure for an irregular heartbeat. He was a young dad and husband. His plan did not include lying on a gurney, wondering if he would ever see his family again. The doctor walked in and explained what was about to take place: "We are going to stop your heart from beating, and when we kick it back on, we hope that it will beat in rhythm again." My friend was scared to undergo the procedure, but the outcome was what he had hoped for— his heart began to beat in rhythm.

God's plan for us is that we live in rhythm with him, in lockstep. All of us need God to reach in at times and restart our hearts to beat in rhythm with him again. Maybe it's through Confession, or Mass, or daily prayer. Maybe it's the Rosary or a men's group. Maybe it's a consecration to St. Joseph or the Blessed Virgin Mary. Maybe God desires that we deal with an addiction by joining Alcoholics Anonymous, Gamblers Anonymous, or Sex Anonymous. Or deal with the past by seeing a counselor. Maybe he inspires us to go on retreat, to disconnect from normal life and reconnect with him. Maybe he wants us to work on our role as a husband or to reengage with our children, no matter their age. Maybe he wants to give us the grace to forgive the person we can't find forgiveness for. Whatever it is, it's time to trust God with your past, present, and future, knowing that he will do miracles in your life and in your heart. One step at a time.

The glossary to the *Catechism of the Catholic Church* defines miracles as "a sign or wonder such as a healing or the control of nature, which can only be attributed to divine power." One miracle attributed to Padre Pio was the healing of a crippled man with clubbed feet. He was a beggar with crutches who couldn't walk or even stand up. One day, as Padre Pio walked by, the man, also named Francesco, yelled out, "Padre Pio, give me a blessing!" Padre Pio looked at him and said, "Throw away your crutches!" The man was stunned. Padre Pio then shouted, "I said, 'Throw away your crutches!'" Padre Pio left the man and walked into church to celebrate Mass. Francesco got up and for the first time began to walk. He was healed. This is one of many miracles attributed to St. Pio. Francesco's plan was to beg for money, never imagining he could be healed, but God's plan for Francesco was to walk.

God's plan is that we get up and walk, too. We are all crippled in some way. We have shortcomings and wounds. But God heals, provides, and delivers a way. It's time for us to throw away our crutches—our excuses and old ways of living—and begin to walk with Christ, to follow his plan.

One step at a time. Each day. Walking in rhythm with God—in lockstep.

ACTION PLAN

1. Make prayer a priority in your daily life. Decide how, when, and where you will pray each day. Don't fret about missing a day; if you do, just restart the next day.

2. What is one way you can allow God to restart your heart? Maybe it could be through attending daily Mass, going to Confession, signing up for a retreat, or joining a men's group. Whatever it is, decide to move forward.

3. How can you align your plans with God's plan for your life? Take some time to reflect on your goals. How does God take the lead? How can you surrender and trust the Lord with your goals?

Prayer of St. Pio of Pietrelcina after Holy Communion

STAY WITH ME, LORD

Stay with me, Lord, for it is necessary to have you present so that I do not forget you. You know how easily I abandon you. Stay with me, Lord, because I am weak and I need your strength, that I may not fall so often. Stay with me, Lord, for you are my life, and without you, I am without fervor. Stay with me, Lord, for you are my light, and without you, I am in darkness. Stay with me, Lord, to show me your will. Stay with me, Lord, so that I hear your voice and follow you. Stay with me, Lord, for I desire to love you very much, and always be in your company. Stay with me, Lord, if you wish me to be faithful to you. Stay with me, Lord, for as poor as my soul is, I want it to be a place of consolation for you, a nest of love. Stay with me, Jesus, for it is getting late and the day is coming to a close, and life passes; death, judgment, eternity approaches. It is necessary to renew my strength, so that I will not stop along the way and for that, I need you. It is getting late and death approaches, I fear the darkness, the temptations, the dryness, the cross, the sorrows. O how I need you, my Jesus, in this night of exile! Stay with me tonight, Jesus, in life with all its dangers. I need you.

Let me recognize you as your disciples did at the breaking of the bread, so that the Eucharistic Communion be the Light which disperses the darkness, the force which sustains me, the unique joy of my heart. Stay with me, Lord, because at the hour of my death, I want to remain united to you, if not by communion, at least by grace and love. Stay with me, Jesus, I do not ask for divine consolation, because I do not merit it, but the gift of your presence, oh yes, I ask this of you! Stay with me, Lord, for it is you alone I look for, your Love, your Grace, your Will, your Heart, your Spirit, because I love you and ask no other reward but to love you more and more. With a firm love, I will love you with all my heart while on earth and continue to love you perfectly during all eternity. Amen.

DISCUSSION/JOURNALING QUESTIONS

1. How does your daily routine allow you to live in rhythm, in lockstep, with God through prayer?

2. What areas of your life are difficult to surrender to God?

3. What is the most difficult part, for you, in trusting God?

4. What are some excuses you use that keep you from living consistently in relationship and in rhythm with God?

5. How do your plans differ from God's plans?

6

BEING RESTORED

Receiving new life in Christ with St. Peter

Born around AD 1, Shimon Bar Yonah (Simon, Son of John/ Jonah) grew up in Bethsaida, a small town on the banks of the Galilee River, about seventy miles from Jerusalem. Simon was a fisherman, a trade he probably learned from his father and grandfather at an early age. Bethsaida, which means "house of fishermen" or "house of hunters," was a blue-collar town whose economy rode on the backs of men who worked on the water. Simon no doubt was gritty, competing as a commercial fisherman in a tough business.

Over two thousand years later, fishermen still make a living doing what Simon did, spending days, nights, and even weeks at a time out on a boat. I live in South Louisiana, where fishing is more than a sport on the inland waterways and on the Gulf Coast. For many, it's the way to support their families. Like Simon, these folks work long, grueling hours, no matter the weather, making a living. Fishing, like farming, can be stressful and is always physically challenging.

We don't know much about Simon's personal life other than that he was married, as scripture tells us he had a mother-in-law. We also know that Simon was a devoted Jew. Like most Jewish men at the time, he followed the customs and practices of his religion. But even with his religious background, Simon was spiritually hungry. He was searching for more, so much so that he was willing to leave his job as a fisherman and follow a rabbi named Jesus.

If you ever spend time on the docks where fishermen come in, dumping their haul of shrimp, oysters, crabs, or fish, you can't help but notice their toughness and their grit. I'm no expert in picking disciples, but I know that if I had been Jesus, I would have picked men with grit. I would have picked men like Simon, who were tough. I'd rally for men with rough edges—men who could work, handle their business, and take risks.

Jesus wasn't concerned with picking the smartest or most talented men. He wasn't looking for men who had a strategic plan, all their goals and objectives set. I don't think Jesus cared whether men were successful in the eyes of society, either. He was no fool. We know that he didn't just randomly pick his disciples out of a hat. No, Jesus was intentional about who he chose. There were no mistakes in his choosing, not even with Judas. Jesus picked men, like Simon, who had grit, because Jesus knew what was to come and what they would have to face.

Simon was one of the first disciples Jesus called. The Gospel of Matthew describes how it happened: "As he was walking by the Sea of Galilee, he saw two brothers, Simon who is called Peter, and his brother Andrew, casting a net into the sea; they were fishermen. He said to them, 'Come after me, and I will make you fishers of men.' At once they left their nets and followed him" (4:18–20). Men with grit take risks, and Simon did just that, casting aside his livelihood to follow

Jesus. Jesus called Simon to more than fishing. Jesus called Simon to new life, a life that Simon longed for but had yet to taste.

Men with grit take risks. Men with holy grit take spiritual risks, leaving behind their old selves and accepting the new life Jesus calls them to. Jesus did not call Simon and the other apostles because they had it all together. No, Jesus chose men with grit, men who were broken, sinners, messy. Over time Jesus taught them how to be men of holy grit.

Simon, who would become the leader of the apostles, was a work in progress. In one account in scripture, the disciples were out in a boat after Jesus went off to pray alone. In the fourth watch of the night, between 3 a.m. and 6 a.m., a storm came through. Jesus approached the boat, walking on the water. The disciples were certain it was a ghost. But as Jesus moved closer, he reassured them: "Take courage, it is I; do not be afraid" (Mt 14:27).

Simon called out and Jesus tested his faith, asking him to step out of the boat and come to him. Risking humiliation, Simon stepped out on the water to walk to Jesus. Maybe he didn't think about it; maybe he was a bit spontaneous, or maybe he was prideful. All we know is that he stepped out of the boat and for one moment walked on water. Then he sank. As described in the Gospel of Matthew, "But when he saw how strong [the wind] was he became frightened; and, beginning to sink, he cried out, 'Lord, save me!' Immediately Jesus stretched out his hand and caught him, and said to him, 'O you of little faith, why did you doubt?'" (14:30–31). This is the man Jesus would invest in. A man who took risks, who had grit, but sank! Simon was certainly a work in progress.

I relate to Simon, because I know without a doubt that I am a work in progress. But Jesus calls me, and you, to leave our nets and follow him. There is risk involved, there is cost, but heaven is the reward; new life is at stake.

Simon had ups and downs, like you and me, but he never quit. Did he deny Jesus? Yep. Did he exert his ego at the wrong time? He did. Did he sink? Yes. Did he put his foot in his mouth? Absolutely. But he fell in love with Jesus, and although he failed often, he never stopped loving Jesus. In our culture today, we see many folks who, when times are hard, quit. Men with grit, men like Simon, don't quit when things get tough. There's a trend of men who quit on faith, who quit on Jesus, who quit on the Church, who quit their marriages. Times are hard, living for Christ isn't easy, the Church isn't perfect—but quitting should not be an option. Men with holy grit are called to lead, to model for others what it means to commit and not give up.

Simon became Peter. Jesus changed his name and gave him the keys to the Church. Peter led the apostles during the most turbulent of times, the persecutions of Christians. Peter expressed his love for Jesus three times (see John 21), thus making up for the three times he had denied Jesus during the Passion. This exchange between Jesus and Peter, which we will talk more about in a moment, is one of the greatest confessions of healing recorded in scripture.

Simon received a new name and new life in Christ. He led the Church to the center of the known world, Rome, and it was there that he was martyred for his faith. Tradition holds that Peter chose to be crucified upside down because he felt unworthy to die the same death as his Lord.

Simon the fisherman became the first pope. Today, we know him as St. Peter the Apostle, and we look to him as a model of sainthood and a man with holy grit.

NEW LIFE

Jesus offers all of us a new life, not just Peter. This is not just a concept or a metaphor; it's real. This is not something that is relative to "my truth." No. Jesus who is truth, reveals himself to you and me and offers us new life. Peter knew that Jesus was offering him a new life. He didn't always get it, but he took the step, risked it, dropped his nets.

In the Gospel of Matthew, we see another important conversation between Jesus and Peter. Jesus asks the disciples, "Who do people say that the Son of Man is?" (16:13). The disciples reply, "Some say John the Baptist, others Elijah, still others Jeremiah or one of the prophets" (v. 14). But Jesus isn't satisfied just hearing what the crowds are saying. He wants to know what they, the disciples, think!

"But who do you say that I am?" he asks (v. 15). Peter responds, "You are the Christ, the Son of the living God" (v. 16). He is the first to proclaim Jesus's identity. Just as he stepped swiftly out of the boat when Jesus called to him, now Peter steps out in faith and speaks the truth boldly. Jesus knew Peter's words were not his own but were anointed by God. Grace flowed in Peter's life and in his heart. Conversion was happening, new life beginning to grow! Not long after this bold statement of faith, however, Peter would deny Jesus.

I'm sure there have been times in your life when there was a disconnect between what you wanted to do and what you did. I'm certain, if you are like me, there have been times when your actions did not turn out the way you intended. This was Peter. This is me. One day Peter was the boldest follower of Christ, and the next day he was the biggest coward.

What I see in Peter is what I see in myself: the ability to go all in, either way. I can forget the "holy" part of holy grit. But Jesus sees in me, and in you, what he saw in Peter. Potential. Goodness. Intentions that need direction. Ambitions that need grace. Brokenness that needs healing. Grittiness that needs a dose of holiness. Jesus spent years helping Peter connect the dots between his heart and his head—between his actions and his thoughts. He helped Peter evolve from a gritty fisherman into a man pursuing holiness. This takes time.

In sacred scripture, God changes people's names as a sign of a covenant, of new beginnings, of new life. The name Abram, which means "exalted father," became Abraham, "father of many nations." His wife Sarai, whose name means "princess," became Sarah, "my princess." Abraham and Sarah both struggled with God's plan for their lives, but God gave them new life and fulfilled his promise of a son, Isaac.

Jacob became Israel. He went from a man who wrestled with God and stole his brother's inheritance to a man in love with God and the leader of a nation.

Saul, a murderer, became Paul. He took on a new name and a new mission in Christ. He never turned back.

And Shimon Bar Yonah became Cephas, translated as Peter ("rock"). Jesus told him, "And so I say to you, you are Peter, and upon this rock I will build my church, and the gates of the netherworld shall not prevail against it. I will give you the keys to the kingdom of heaven" (vv. 18–19). Peter's God-given name, Rock, signified his relationship with Christ, his identity in Christ, and his mission to serve Christ.

God gives us a new name and a new life, too. At baptism, our name is called out as God claims us as his sons. At Confirmation, we choose our own name, often the name of a saint. Maybe you didn't do that, or you can't remember, but it's a sign that through Christ we are given new life and a new mission, which is to be a saint with grit.

On a deep spiritual level, God wants to speak to you and me as he spoke to Peter, calling us to leave our old name (self) behind and embrace our new name (new life) in him. He invites us to a new relationship with him, to grasp our identity as his beloved son, and to find our mission by serving him in the places he plants us.

AN INVITATION

"Do you love me?" Jesus asked (Jn 21:16).

There are some questions in life that require an answer. More than twenty-five years ago, when I stood face-to-face with my future wife in front of the altar, the priest asked me to say my vows. "Do you, Paul, take Gretchen to be your wife? Do you promise to love and honor her all the days of your life?" These vows required a yes or no response. In front of everyone, I had to state my intentions. Yes or no.

Sounds elementary, but it's not. These vows are lifelong, forever. These vows are not easy, they are often hard. Did I fully know what I was committing to at the time? Sort of, but not fully. The longer we've been married, going through the ups and downs, the more I realize how real the covenant I made was. Our yes, our vows, our commitment means something, and it's real, everyday.

There is no easy way around a covenant promise. It is what it is. Husband and wife make a covenant commitment to each other by stating their vows. Have I ever wanted to give up, quit on my vows? Yep. Do I want to take the easy road sometimes? Yes, I do. My fallen nature wants to give up when things are hard. Sometimes I don't want to do the tough things, the hard work.

Peter often tried to take the easy way out, the quickest way there. At times he got in his own way. It's our nature to want to take the easy road. I notice this in my own life. The Israelites did this too as they tried to reach the Promised Land. God rerouted them instead. The miracle of the Red Sea was more important than a shorter route.

God takes us the holy way, not the easy way. He's more concerned with our conversion than with our comfort. My new self, the new life God has given me, moves me to push through the fog and stay focused on the goal of loving my bride forever.

A husband and wife seal the vows they have taken by giving themselves totally to each other, offering their bodies to one another. It's not just words that make the vows a reality, but a sacrifice of total self. The covenants in the Old Testament, God's promises, were signed, sealed, and delivered by offering a sacrifice. The blood of sacrificed lambs painted on the doorposts of the Israelites was a sign of God's promise. Jesus fulfilled the promise of the Father by signing the covenant with his life; being sacrificed on the Cross, he painted his own blood on the doorposts of our souls. God's promises are never broken, and the blood of Jesus has forever set us free.

Jesus asked Peter some very important questions. He asked him to take vows, to make a promise. But more importantly, he asked Peter to make a covenant with him. A promise can be broken, but a covenant is a sign of giving everything—your heart, your life.

Peter made his covenant with Christ at the Sea of Tiberias (known today as the Sea of Galilee) after Jesus's Crucifixion, Death, and Resurrection. Jesus and Peter were having breakfast together, sitting around a charcoal fire, when Jesus asked Peter three questions. Many theologians have attested that these questions were not only a steppingstone for the future but also an opportunity to give Peter a "redo." Peter had denied Jesus three times during the most agonizing episode of his life. Out of fear, Peter had bailed. So did almost everyone else, except John, Mary, and Jesus's mother, Mary. On the beaches of Galilee, Peter now has the opportunity to own up to his earlier actions and make up for them. He can look at Jesus and say, *I'm sorry. I failed.* Confession isn't a time for self-hatred, but a time for self-reflection and healing. The Sacrament of Reconciliation is an opportunity for us to look into the loving eyes of Jesus and say, *I'm sorry, I'm imperfect, I failed, and I need you.*

One of the breakthroughs in my marriage happened this way. It was an honest conversation with my wife, who looked at me and said, "I feel like you don't need me." At the time, I would occasionally say, "I don't 'need' you," which meant that I was fine being self-sufficient. This attitude of course was coming from my pride and a broken place in me that swore that I didn't "need" anyone, that I could do it all myself. But marriage is about total vulnerability, letting the other person in. And there were places in my heart that I hadn't yet opened. After that conversation, I began to acknowledge that I "needed" my wife—not to cook or fold my clothes, although those things are fine—but that I "needed" her to love me and to see me for who I really am. That's when we began to take the next step in our relationship.

Before Jesus left his disciples in bodily form, he gave Peter an opportunity to express his sorrow by "redoing" his denial. He gave Peter an opening to admit his need for Jesus to give him new life. The *Catechism of the Catholic Church* says, "Christ liberates us from sin; by his Resurrection, he opens for us the way to a new life. This new life is above all justification that reinstates us in God's grace, 'so that as Christ was raised from the dead by the glory of the Father, we too might walk in newness of life.' Justification consists in both victory over the death caused by sin and a new participation in grace. It brings about filial adoption so that men become Christ's brethren, as Jesus himself called his disciples after his Resurrection" (para. 654).

Jesus asked Peter, "Simon, son of John, do you love me more than these?" Peter responded, "Yes, Lord, you know that I love you" (Jn 21:15). Jesus asked him again, "Simon, son of John do you love me?" (v. 16). Again, Peter says yes. Then "[Jesus] said to him the third time, 'Simon, son of John, do you love me?'" (v. 17). Peter had freedom to say yes or no to Jesus's questions. No one forced him to say yes, just as no one forced me to stand in front of the altar on my wedding day and say yes to my bride. I went freely. When Peter had this conversation with Jesus, he came freely.

Peter felt sorrow in response to Jesus's insistent questioning: "Peter was distressed that he had said to him a third time, 'Do you love me?'" (v. 17). This distress was a sign of his heartfelt contrition. Peter responded, "Lord, you know everything; you know that I love you" (v. 17). In this interaction with Christ, three things took place. First, Peter's relationship with Jesus was restored. Second, Peter was reminded of his identity as God's son. The prodigal son had returned—that was Peter, and it's you and me. Third, Peter was given his mission to live for Christ. Jesus said to him, "Feed my sheep" (v. 17). Peter was restored. He was given new life, again.

The invitation for you and for me is to be restored to new life in Christ. Our yes is the start, and when we fail, we must get up and say yes again. "Lord, I'm sorry. Lord, I need you!"

We made a covenant with Christ at our baptism. Christ made a new covenant for us with God the Father through his death on the Cross. That covenant is renewed on the altar at every Mass, through every Eucharist. Just as Jesus asked Peter, "Do you love me?" he asks us the same question. Our response is our covenant with him. Will we fail? Yep. Will we fall short? Certainly. But Jesus gives us, like Peter, new chances to get back up and follow him daily. Like St. Peter, let us be restored in Christ and say yes to the new life Jesus offers us.

ACTION PLAN

1. Create an action plan for your relationship with Christ:

Peter's relationship with Jesus was restored, over and again. Take some time to think about how you can improve your relationship with Christ. What is hindering you from being close to him? This is a good time to go to Reconciliation or to get away on retreat.

2. Create an action plan for your identity:

Peter was reminded of his identity in Christ. Prayer is essential in allowing Jesus to speak to us. How can your prayer life become more vibrant and active? Maybe begin by saying the Rosary more often, reading scripture more, or taking quiet time each day to reflect on the Gospel readings. Our identity, the truth of who we are, is also spoken to us by others. Find trusted people who can speak truth into your life and remind you who you are in Christ.

3. Create an action plan for your mission:

Peter was given his mission by Christ. How is Christ inviting you to serve him and others in your life? Does your parish need volunteers? Does your diocese need help? Consider what your gifts are and what's on your heart; then investigate opportunities for service in the Church.

Prayer to St. Peter

O Holy Apostle, you are the Rock upon which Almighty God has built his Church. Obtain for me, I pray you: lively faith, firm hope, and burning love, complete detachment from myself, contempt of the world, patience in adversity, humility in prosperity, recollection in prayer, purity of heart, a right intention in all my works, diligence in fulfilling the duties of

my state of life, constancy in my resolutions, resignation to
the will of God, and perseverance in the grace of God even
unto death; that so, by means of your intercession and your
glorious merits, I may be made worthy to appear before the
Chief and Eternal Shepherd of Souls, Jesus Christ, who with
the Father and the Holy Spirit lives and reigns forever. Amen.
   and:

   Thou art the shepherd of the sheep, the Prince of the Apostles, unto thee were given the keys of the kingdom of heaven.
"Thou art Peter; and upon this rock I will build my Church."
Raise us up, we beseech thee, O Lord, by the apostolic assis-
tance of blessed Peter, thine apostle; so that the weaker we are,
the more mightily we may be helped by the power of his intercession; and that being perpetually defended by the same holy
apostle, we may neither yield to any iniquity, nor be overcome
by any adversity. Through Christ, Our Lord. Amen.

DISCUSSION/JOURNALING QUESTIONS

1. In what ways, like Peter, have you fallen in your walk with
   Christ?

2. How is God inviting you to respond to him, to be restored?

3. What are some things that hold you back from experiencing the new life that Christ offers you?

4. How are you related to St. Peter, in both his old ways and
   his new ways of living?

7

LOVE AT FIRST SIGHT

Abiding in God's love with St. Maximilian Kolbe

Maximilian Kolbe is one of the most revered saints of our time. We admire his selfless actions and the sacrificial love that cost him his life. His impact upon the world continues to be felt to this day.

Raymund Kolbe was born in Poland in 1894 during a tumultuous time in history, when his country was part of the Russian empire and Poland sought its independence. Unrest simmered throughout Europe, and Raymund faced much adversity growing up and throughout his life.

Many say that the grittiest people come out of suffering and hardships. That was Raymund. When he was twenty, his father was captured and executed for defending Polish independence. We will talk about another great saint in a later chapter who also came from adversity in Poland, St. John Paul II.

Despite everything Raymund and his family went through, they had faith. Raymund had fallen in love with Jesus at an early age, and his devotion to the Blessed Virgin

Mary was a catalyst for his deep love for Christ and his calling to enter religious life. At the age of thirteen, Raymund
left home illegally with his older brother and crossed the bor-
der into Austria-Hungry. There they entered the Conventual
Franciscan seminary in Lwów. In 1910, Raymund joined the
novitiate and was given the religious name Maximilian.

Those who have heard of Maximilian Kolbe often point
to the heroics at the end of his life, but there's more. He was a
man on a mission, a missionary with a purpose. Friar Maximilian was set on reaching as many people as he could with
the Good News of Jesus. After nine years away from his home,
he returned as a newly ordained priest to bring Jesus to independent Poland. His deep love of God was rooted in the faith
and the sacraments.

Kolbe said, "The most deadly poison of our times is indifference. And this happens, although the praise of God should
know no limits. Let us strive, therefore, to praise him to the
greatest extent of our powers." Apathy. Mediocrity. Lukewarmness. Kolbe believed this indifference kept people from
experiencing the abundant life of Jesus. God the Father speaks
about this in Revelation: "I know your works; I know that you
are neither cold nor hot. I wish you were either cold or hot.
So, because you are lukewarm, neither hot nor cold, I will spit
you out of my mouth" (3:15–16). Indifference and a false sense
of self-sufficiency are the root causes of our failure to give our
total self to God.

Indifference was around during the time of Jesus, it was
prevalent during the time of Kolbe, and it's still a problem
today. When we search our hearts, we see it. Any time we
don't want to respond to love, we turn away, ignore the invitation, be indifferent. When apathy creeps in, we lose touch
with who we are and what our purpose is. Marriages fail when
indifference seeps into our hearts. Our faith begins to subside
when we become lukewarm. We distance ourselves from love,

from our own family, when we subscribe to mediocrity. The Church loses its mission when lukewarmness lingers.

I know this to be true for myself. When I'm indifferent, apathetic, or lukewarm about something, I stop caring about it. Maybe it's my health or my marriage or my faith life or my job or my kids or my friendships; but truth be told, when I'm lukewarm I am not living abundantly.

Friar Kolbe discovered that falling in love with Jesus meant fighting the temptation to settle for mediocrity. His relationship with Mother Mary motivated him to fight lukewarmness. When he saw a need, a place that was empty in his heart, he allowed God to love him, saying, "a single act of love makes a soul return to life." This was his goal—for his soul to be in love and alive with God. He wanted others to experience this, too. During his first arrest by the Nazis, he said to those with him, "Courage, my sons. Don't you see that we are leaving on a mission? They pay our fare in the bargain. What a piece of good luck! The thing to do now is to pray well in order to win as many souls as possible." He saw his arrest as an opportunity. His love for Jesus moved him past apathy, to mission!

When Kolbe saw a need in his friary, he responded to it. At the start of his assignment in Poland, there were about eighteen friars in his community. This number eventually grew to 650, making it the largest Catholic religious house in Europe. When Kolbe saw an opportunity in his community, he again sought to do something. He began publishing a monthly magazine to spread the Good News. The magazine grew in popularity, eventually reaching one million people. He started a radio broadcast, sending over the radio waves the hope of Jesus to a war-torn region. And when he saw a need that stretched beyond his capacity, he allowed God to take control and lead him.

Maximilian spent six years in Japan as a missionary. He started an outreach ministry in Nagasaki, one of the cities hit by an atomic bomb in 1945. The mission base was placed on the side of a mountain, which protected it from the bomb. Maximilian accomplished all these things not knowing where God would lead him next. Little did he know that his work was preparing him for his most heroic act of love.

Kolbe said, "Let us remember that love lives through sacrifice and is nourished by giving. . . . Without sacrifice there is no love." One cannot extract sacrifice from love and still call it love. The two coexist. Any meaningful relationship I have requires sacrifice. It requires me to give my total self. Without that, love falls short. To fall in love brings with it the willingness to give everything, to make changes, to do things we never thought possible—to sacrifice. Kolbe lived out this kind of love every day. But this wasn't a love that was self-driven; the love that Kolbe had overflowed from his total gift of himself to Jesus. Jesus loved him and loved through him.

Kolbe and his brother friars fed and housed thousands of refugees during World War II, people of all faiths and backgrounds. When Kolbe spoke out against the evil of the Nazi regime, he was arrested for the second time on February 17, 1941, and sent to Auschwitz concentration camp. He was branded a prisoner, #16670. Kolbe was treated horrifically, often beaten and tortured, yet he remained faithful to Jesus.

In July of 1941, a prisoner escaped from the camp. As punishment, the commander picked ten men to starve to death in a bunker. Upon hearing that he was one of those chosen, Franciszek Gajowniczek cried out, "My wife! My children!" At that point Maximilian Kolbe stepped up and without hesitation asked to take the place of Franciszek, which the guard allowed. Kolbe spent weeks slowly starving to death in an underground cell. He committed himself to praying for each of the other men as they died. The guards finally executed Kolbe by lethal injection. Friar Maximilian Kolbe was forty-six.

Word spread of Fr. Kolbe's heroism, love, and sacrifice. Many miracles happened, too. Franciszek survived his imprisonment and would later give testimony to Kolbe's life and be present at his canonization in 1982. During the canonization ceremony, Pope John Paul II said, "Maximilian did not die, but gave his life for his brother." Kolbe gave everything. Today, he is known as St. Maximilian Kolbe, the patron saint of the twentieth century.

FALLING IN LOVE

What is more difficult, falling in love or staying in love? I've had this question posed to me a few times. The soul awakens when one falls in love. My soul awoke when I fell in love with my wife. Falling in love was easy. Sure, I had some fears and doubts, but as soon as I let go of those, I fell hard.

My soul awoke too when I gave my life to Jesus. I surrendered. I had questions, doubts, and fears, but once I let go of those, my heart fell in love and broke open. My outlook changed overnight, but changes in my behavior and attitudes took time. I'm still on the journey of healing, growth, and conversion. Love requires more of us than falling. It's the day-to-day process of loving that develops holy grit within us.

We all know the feeling when the romance wears off and disillusionment sets in. The reality is that loving takes work. I remember the day I woke up not long after our wedding and thought, *This is a lot harder than I realized.* I had to choose to be married that day, choose to love. I remember, also, when my initial conversion wore off, and my old ways, old temptations, began to lure me back in. I began to think, *Loving God is hard.* That day, I had to choose to love. I remember when my children were born, being so in love with the little bundles in my arms; then later, waking up in the middle of the night to change a diaper or clean up puke, thinking, *I don't want to do this right now.* Or when they got older and I'd be up after midnight, worried until they came home safely. I had to choose to love. We've all been there.

Choosing to love is difficult. It takes grit and effort. Love is ultimately not a feeling, although there are times when we "feel" in love. But many days, love is a choice, it's a decision to put another person first, to sacrifice. Choosing, deciding, sacrificing—these all go together.

I'm certain that the day St. Maximilian took the place of another man in that starvation bunker he didn't "feel" like doing it. I'm certain he didn't have the joy or excitement he probably experienced on the day he was ordained to the priesthood. I'm certain that his mind and heart weren't feeling passionate about the thought of starving to death. No, what went through his mind and heart was a decision to love and sacrifice for the sake of something greater—a man's life and his family.

Our souls remain awake when we stay in love. And God wants our souls to remain alert and alive. Jesus speaks of this when he says, "I am the true vine" (Jn 15:1). He goes on, "Remain in me, as I remain in you. Just as a branch cannot bear fruit on its own unless it remains on the vine, so neither can you unless you remain in me. I am the vine, you are the branches" (Jn 15:4–5). He asks us to remain, to abide, in him. This is love.

Jesus is not just giving us a suggestion or good advice. Jesus is giving us truth, facts, and a road map to follow. Some versions of scripture interchange the words "abide" and "remain," calling us to stay connected, to not break away from the vine. Abide and remain.

Jesus continues, "Without me you can do nothing" (v. 5). This is God telling us how to live abundantly. This is what we all want, to be fully alive, right? Abiding. Remaining. Don't we all desire to stay in love? This might be the greatest accomplishment of our life. If someone were to say a few words about you at a memorial service, which statement would have more impact: "He fell in love" or "He stayed in love his whole life"? No one is remembered for falling in love; they are remembered for staying in love. The act of loving each day is our mission, our purpose. It's what Jesus calls us to do; even more, what we are commanded to do, commissioned to do. We are all called to be like St. Maximilian Kolbe.

What does it look like for men to fall in love and stay in love with Jesus? How can a man pursue God with his whole heart and his whole life? In Maximilian's case, he chose to stand in the place of a young father, giving up his life out of love for Christ. Jesus said, "No one has greater love than this, to lay down one's life for one's friends" (Jn 15:13).

Kolbe always wanted to be a soldier. He was gritty. He desired to fight, to defend the weak and protect his sovereign country. God had other plans, calling Kolbe to be a spiritual warrior, a priest with grit. And in one of his greatest moments, he did what any soldier would do, give his life for another—just as Jesus did. Sacrificial love is what makes us great, holy, gritty. Men are made for this kind of love! This is where the rubber meets the road, where we gain traction, make an impact, find our purpose, and catch our wind!

When I have sacrificed for someone else, I have not looked back or felt empty. My heart remained full when I loved as Jesus loved. I never have regrets when I serve or give. When I love sacrificially, my heart is full. That's because I'm living the way God created me to live!

Yet the opposite is true too. When I'm selfish, when I'm living for me, things go south fast. Fog sets in. Life becomes cloudy. Disillusionment takes over, and I begin to see my wife, my kids, the Church, others, even God, differently. I start to backslide, and my eyes and heart begin to say that maybe something else will suffice. Nah! Not true!

St. Maximilian Kolbe once said, "The Cross is the school of love." If we want to learn how to be men of holy grit, we must look to the Cross, the altar of sacrifice where Jesus gave his life for his friends (you and me). St. Maximilian lived this out in his vocation. Was he perfect? No. But he was faithful to Christ, and from the heart the mouth speaks, actions come to fruition. When it came time for Kolbe to act like Jesus, he did just that. And we are still talking about him today, the simple man who took the place of another.

I have a friend who as an adult changed his name to Max, after St. Maximilian. Crazy, I know. It's a long story, but at one point during a rough time in his journey, he began to feel connected to St. Maximilian. He told me that Kolbe was instrumental to his deeper conversion, that Kolbe was "fearless and faithful. . . . despite suffering through incredible darkness, he was a reflection of God's light, and led with a life of wild abandon—as Mother Teresa puts it, 'an absolute, unconditional and unwavering confidence in God our loving Father, even when everything seems to be a total failure.'"

I pressed him to tell me more about how St. Maximilian Kolbe gave him the hope to move forward. He replied, "I have suffered through some very dark times (unfortunately still do), but St. Maximilian Kolbe's example gives me strength to remain faithful, and his intercession brings me God's grace to battle fear. And more and more I am turning fear to faith and confidence. Even when everything seems a total failure, I find joy. In the present moments, at home and at work, I have the courage to stop doubting and being discouraged, but instead to walk in that freedom, with wild abandon."

"Wild abandon" describes St. Maximilian's life. Those two words sound a little odd, but think about it. A man of grit is a wild man, a courageous man. A man of holiness is an abandoned man, a man who is all in—in love. Kolbe was courageously all in. He was connected to the Vine, Jesus! He remained and abided till the end.

AN INVITATION

This is a bold statement, but hear me out: Every man needs an amazing woman to help him find true love.

Men have their gifts. God created us unique and designed us with a purpose. But we also have our faults; we can be stubborn and prideful. Our heads can get in the way of our hearts. Women, however, through God's wonderful design, have a unique intuition to give and receive love. Men and women complement each other; thus man without woman and woman without man just isn't complete.

When men and women are at odds, they turn away from each other and from God. We see this clearly in our world. We saw it with Adam and Eve hiding in the garden, naked, blaming each other. However, when man and woman love as God designed, when they love like Jesus, they turn toward the other. They complement each other. Their love shines bright to the world, showing everyone what true love looks like.

Through her natural gifts, a good mother nurtures love in her children. A father's love is also extremely important, but a mother's love has a unique influence on her children. A loving wife receives love and breaks through her husband's hard shell. A wife's love often draws man beyond himself, so that he holds himself accountable to be his best self. Male friendships are vital too, but the uniqueness of a woman's love is a reality that cannot be overstated. Adam was incomplete without Eve, and she without him. Creation was missing something before woman came to be. Man and woman need each other to more fully radiate true, authentic love—God's love.

St. Maximilian Kolbe was in love with a woman, too: the Blessed Virgin Mary. She, the mother of Jesus, is the most perfect of all women. And she, unlike any other human being, loved her son above all. Her love was perfect. As a priest, and even before his ordination, Kolbe dedicated his life to Mary. He had a deep devotion to her, he loved her, and she loved him.

St. Maximilian Kolbe's great love for Jesus impelled him to heroically sacrifice his life for his neighbor. We may wonder how he achieved such love for Christ. I believe that Mary showed Maximilian how to love her son! Maximilian's heavenly mother drew him close to Jesus. Maximilian's life's work—his ministry, priesthood, and mission—was devoted to the Blessed Virgin, whom he referred to as Immaculata. He started Militia Immaculata (MI), a mission to bring souls to Christ through Mary. Mary, the perfect saint, the God-bearer, teaches us how to fall in love and stay in love.

Many years ago, I was meeting with a young adult man who was struggling with an addiction to pornography. Over time we prayed, set up accountability, and he went to Confession and Mass. Things got better, but he continued to struggle, and it was painful for him. He desired freedom. Yet the shame of this particular sin made him feel unlovable, even by God. He couldn't fathom that God could love him. Of course, this wasn't true, but the shame he carried was strong. Call it bondage.

We were both feeling frustrated, and during our last meeting, as a last-ditch effort, we asked the Blessed Virgin Mary to help this young man be set free. I sat there, praying with him. Soon, he began to cry. His eyes closed as he prayed, tears rolling down his face. I was taken aback, wondering what was going on. He had never shown any emotion when we met other than deep shame. His heart had been closed. But at this particular moment, something broke inside of him. I leaned in and asked, "What's happening?" He said, "As I was praying, I saw Mary come close to me, grab my hand, look me in the eyes, and tell me she loved me. She picked me up as a mother would a child and brought me to the arms of Jesus." We were both in awe. That was it; he was set free. Mother Mary brought him to Jesus, and he was released from the prison of shame, through Mary. He now had the grace to allow Jesus to love him in his shame.

St. Maximilian Kolbe said, "I felt the Immaculata drawing me to herself more and more closely. . . . I had a custom of keeping a holy picture of one of the Saints to whom she appeared on my prie-dieu in my cell, and I used to pray to the Immaculata very fervently." Mother Mary (Immaculata) was with him always, even in prison.

I had never really thought about or tapped into the love of Mother Mary until I witnessed this young man's experience. From there I began to search more and discovered that Mary helps us to become the men we most desire to be. Like any good woman, she helps us to love—but even more than that, Mary purifies our love as the spouse of the Holy Spirit and the beloved mother of Jesus. I also discovered that we can dedicate our life to Mary through an act of consecration or by simply asking her to take our life into her hands. She is always at our side, just as she never left the side of her son.

St. Maximilian Kolbe stayed in love with Jesus through the ups and downs of his life. He remained faithful despite great suffering. How? He had the Blessed Virgin Mary, the New Eve, the Mother of God, to help him abide and stay connected to the Vine. She helped him fall in love and stay in love with Jesus.

ACTION PLAN

1. St. Maximilian Kolbe said, "The Immaculate alone has from God the promise of victory over Satan. She seeks souls that will consecrate themselves entirely to her, that will become in her hands forceful instruments for the defeat of Satan and the spread of God's kingdom." Prayerfully consider making an act of total consecration to Mary. There are many books and other resources that can prepare and guide us through this important prayer. Here are two:

   ○ *33 Days to Morning Glory*, by Fr. Michael E. Gaitley

   ○ *Behold the Handmaid of the Lord*, by Edward Looney

2. Think of three to five people who you can surround yourself with on a regular basis that challenge you to love, fall in love, and stay in love with Jesus.

3. Write out a plan, some specific goals, about how you can be more loving and courageous like St. Maximilian Kolbe.

Prayer to St. Maximilian Kolbe

St. Maximilian Mary Kolbe, most faithful son of St. Francis, the beggar of Assisi, inflamed with love for God, you journeyed through life practicing heroic virtues and performing true apostolic deeds.

Turn your gaze on us who honor you and have recourse to you.

Radiating with the light of the Immaculate Virgin, you brought countless souls to holiness and introduced them to various apostolic endeavors for the victory of good over evil and to thereby extend the Kingdom of God throughout the whole world.

Obtain for us the light and the strength we need to do good and to bring many souls to Christ.

Perfectly conformed and united with Jesus Christ, our Lord and Savior, you achieved such a high degree of love of neighbor that you were able to freely offer your life in exchange for a fellow prisoner in witness of true evangelical charity.

Beg the Lord on our behalf that, filled with the same fire of love, our faith and good example might also bring others to Christ and secure for us the reward of everlasting life, where we shall praise him together with you in eternal glory. Amen.

Kolbean Prayer to Mary, Mother of the Church

Mary, Mother of the Church, I come before you in the spirit of St. Maximilian Kolbe, who consecrated his Franciscan life and work to you without reserve. You accepted Maximilian's self-offering; accept me. You led Maximilian to Christ; lead me. You formed Maximilian into a mirror of Christ; form me. Your union with Maximilian provided the backdrop for his works of evangelization and heroic acts of charity.

Please grant, through the intercession of St. Maximilian, that I might fully collaborate with you and the Holy Spirit as an instrument for the upbuilding of Christ's Church. Amen.

DISCUSSION/JOURNALING QUESTIONS

1. What is more difficult for you, to fall in love with God or to stay in love with him?

2. In what areas of your life do you find it difficult to live well on a consistent basis?

3. Who in your life challenges you to love the way God desires you to love?

4. How is God inviting you to be more courageous in your life?

8

HOLY GRIT

Seeing clearly with St. Paul

We are all called to be gritty and holy men, yet we are all different. Following Jesus doesn't put us into a mold. We don't lose our personality, our individuality, or our strengths and gifts. Peter was different from Paul, and that's good. Ignatius was different from Augustine, and the world is better for it. Paul speaks about this when he says, "As a body is one though it has many parts, and all the parts of the body, though many, are one body, so also Christ" (1 Cor 12:12). Paul was his own person, and he wasn't afraid to be himself—to be who God made him to be. However, like many of us, it took Paul time to find his true identity.

Paul was born Saul of Tarsus, a city in what is now known as Turkey, around 4–6 BC. Saul had Jewish parents and Roman citizenship. Tradition holds that Saul studied and learned the Torah and eventually moved to Jerusalem, where he became a Pharisee. Pharisees were religious experts and teachers in the Jewish faith who were meant to hold true to the traditions of their beliefs. Jesus too was a practicing Jew, well-versed in the Torah (scripture), and he knew and held true to Jewish traditions. Jesus had many interactions with the Pharisees, who were extreme in their adherence to the rules and laws. Ultimately, they would be the ones to send Jesus to trial and to his death.

We may picture Saul as a religious man who sat in the Temple teaching all day. But that was not the case. Many, if not most, of the Pharisees had day jobs. They worked to provide for their families, like you and me. Saul was a craftsman who worked with his hands as a tentmaker. Tent making was an occupation that took vision and design. It required skills in engineering and architecture, as well as contracting. This was a good job, paying well for skilled labor. Saul would lean on this trade throughout his life to provide a decent income.

As a Pharisee, Saul desired to know God, to live in truth, and to obey the teachings of his faith. You might say Saul had a heart for God even before his conversion. Yet Saul became so hardened and hell-bent on the dictates of the Law that his heart grew to be like stone. He was rigid and cold, all in the name of God. Jesus makes note of this quality when he responds to the Pharisees who question him about marriage. He says that Moses allowed divorce "because of the hardness of your hearts" (Mt 19:8).

Because of his "hardness of heart," Saul became one of the first Pharisees to persecute Christians, particularly Jewish people who believed Jesus was the Christ. Scripture says, "Saul, meanwhile, was trying to destroy the church; entering house after house and dragging out men and women, he handed them over for imprisonment" (Acts 8:3). He was driven and angry, working to eliminate any threat to Jewish law. God, however, saw something great in Saul. He saw in Saul what he sees in all of us: a man with a good heart who desired to do the right thing. But we can't hide anything from God. He also saw in Saul a heart that had become calloused and stony.

God didn't give up on Saul. He continued to seek Saul, to break his heart open and render it his. God knew he could take the same passion Saul had for persecuting Christians and use it to spread the Good News. And he did! Likewise, God · can take us, and our intentions, and use them for good.

Saul was on a journey to arrest and imprison Christians when God intervened. He broke Saul's hardened heart. Scripture says, "On his journey, as he was nearing Damascus, a light from the sky suddenly flashed around him. He fell to the ground and heard a voice saying to him, 'Saul, Saul, why are you persecuting me?' He said, 'Who are you, sir?' The reply came, 'I am Jesus, whom you are persecuting'" (Acts 9:3–5).

Losing his sight, Saul was ushered into the city, where he would remain blind for three days. Call it a silent retreat of sorts. God had Saul's attention. God slowed Saul down and stopped him long enough to take his stony heart and recraft it into something new. Ezekiel explains God's promise: "I will give you a new heart, and a new spirit I will put within you. I will remove the heart of stone from your flesh and give you a heart of flesh. I will put my spirit within you" (36:26–27).

Saul was in the business of tent making and, at the same time, fulfilling the role of a persecutor. But God is in the business of remaking hearts and fulfilling the role of a lover. God does not underestimate the importance of the heart, nor should we. Saul was blind for three days. He learned that seeing with his eyes was not as important as learning to see with his heart.

Our vision is connected to our heart and our soul. We will never see clearly if our heart isn't aligned with God's truth. It will always remain foggy. If we have lust in our heart, our eyes will see lustfully. If we have hatred in our heart, our eyes will see with hatred. If we carry shame in our heart, our eyes will see ourselves in shame. If we have selfishness in our heart, we will see ourselves at the center of everything. Our heart and our soul are at the forefront of our vision, our "seeing." God wants to do in us what he did in Saul—to remake our heart, to give us a new and fresh start, a new life. God wants us to see clearly.

Days after Saul was struck blind, God sent Ananias to him. Laying his hands on Saul, Ananias said, "'Saul, my brother, the Lord has sent me, Jesus who appeared to you on the way by which you came, that you may regain your sight and be filled with the holy Spirit.' Immediately things like scales fell from his eyes and he regained his sight. He got up and was baptized" (Acts 9:17–18). Scales fell from his eyes, and rocks fell from his heart. Saul, now a disciple of Jesus, could see clearly the life God wanted him to live.

You might be thinking that you've never had a moment like Saul—a powerful, immediate conversion. God approaches us all differently in order to break through our hardness of heart. He knows what we need. I'm certain that if you step back and look at your life, you can point to moments, opportunities, and situations when God "knocked you off your horse." I can. Most of my conversion moments are small, but if I add them all together over the course of my life, they create an amazing picture. God will never stop initiating those moments to catch your attention and renew your heart.

Saul could have gone back to his old ways as a respected Pharisee. He could have written off what happened as dumb luck or a mountaintop experience or a "retreat high." He could have forgotten about it. But he didn't. The day after his sight was restored, he began to preach about Jesus in the very places where he once persecuted those who did the same.

Saul the Pharisee would become Paul the evangelist, preaching and sharing the Gospel throughout the Roman Empire from AD 33 to 64. It was common for people of his background to have two names, Saul being his Jewish name and Paul being his Roman name. It is only fitting that he would go by his Roman name once his new life in Christ began, as God would send Paul to preach to the Gentiles (non-Jewish people). Eventually Paul was arrested and imprisoned in Rome during a time of tremendous Christian persecution. Tradition holds that Paul was executed in AD 64, and because he was a Roman citizen, he was brought outside the city walls to be beheaded.

A church named St. Paul's Outside the Walls was built where he died, and it still stands today. St. Paul will forever be known as one of the greatest evangelists of all time, a man who had holy grit.

MAKING TENTS

In my mind I often imagine St. Paul as a gladiator dressed for battle, a warrior on a mission. He had fight in him, both before his conversion and afterward. He was the epitome of a man with grit. Paul traveled during a time when travel was difficult. Three times he was shipwrecked and stranded in unknown territory. He was also arrested, then set free, again and again, only to continue the mission God set before him.

Paul said about his adventures, "Five times at the hands of the Jews I received forty lashes minus one. Three times I was beaten with rods, once I was stoned, three times I was shipwrecked, I passed a night and a day on the deep; on frequent journeys, in dangers from rivers, danger from robbers, dangers from my own race, dangers from Gentiles, dangers in the city, dangers in the wilderness" (2 Cor 11:24–26). Maybe it's just me, but there is something about the life of Paul that is inspiring, that reinvigorates a place in my heart.

St. Paul lived the adventure. There is something innate in a man's heart that desires and seeks adventure. Men are made for it. I speak to many men who are bored and lonely; they go to work, go home, then "rinse and repeat" day after day. They, we, have lost sight of our purpose and our mission. We desire adventure, often not realizing that it's right in front of us. We have a battle to fight—the battle to reclaim our true hearts, to live the adventure God has designed us for!

St. Paul urges us to "persevere in running the race that lies before us while keeping our eyes fixed on Jesus, the leader and perfecter of faith" (Heb 12:1–2). This is our motto, too, our anthem—to run the race, our eyes set on the goal. The prize is Jesus.

Paul was a regular guy, a tentmaker, who was used by God. Paul embraced the specific mission and calling that God chose for him. We can all learn from St. Paul, but we can't be Paul. He was unique, and so are you. You, I, and St. Paul share the same universal call to love God and our neighbor. But how we as individuals live out that call is very different. The *Catechism of the Catholic Church* says, "All Christians in any state or walk of life are called to the fullness of Christian life and to the perfection of charity" (para. 2013). We are all called to holiness: "So be perfect, just as your heavenly Father is perfect" (Mt 5:48). However, we all have different gifts and personalities, and God uses us specifically and uniquely.

Through baptism, you and I are God's sons. We are called to live for him, to love him, and to order our lives with him at the center. St. Paul did this. He lived with God as the center. He was not perfect. And neither are we. St. Paul said, "If I must boast, I will boast of the things that show my weakness" (2 Cor 11:30). St. Paul also realized that it was in his weakness that God did his greatest work: "Where sin increased, grace overflowed all the more" (Rom 5:20). If you and me, like Paul, don't understand our need for God, our spiritual lives will remain in a rut; we'll be stuck.

Self-reliance removes the air from our spiritual lungs. Yet when we lean on God and cling to him, our hearts are filled and we can breathe again. Through daily prayer we connect with God, allowing our conversation with him to recharge our batteries and put air in our tires. As God's sons, we were baptized into Christ's office and ministry as priests, prophets, and kings.

Bishop Robert Barron said, "According to Catholic theology, baptism is much more than merely a symbolic sign of belonging to the church. It is the means by which a person is incorporated into Christ, becoming a member of his mystical body. Baptism, accordingly, makes the baptized an alter Christus, another Christ." As priests we are called to be holy, as prophets we are called to speak the truth, and as kings we are called to lead others to God. This is our mission—to be priest, prophet, and king in our daily lives.

In addition to this universal mission, we each have a specific calling, our individual mission. This is our primary vocation. It is primary because it's the highest in rank of importance in our life. There is nothing more important that you and I can do than to live out, to its fullest, our vocation! If you are married, if you are a priest, if you are living as a single person—this is the place God calls you to be fully alive.

Envy is a dangerous temptation of the enemy—to look at someone else's life and think, *I wish that was me.* The enemy will attack your vocation by spewing lies, tempting you to look somewhere else for happiness, encouraging you to think, *Maybe there's a better, happier vocation than the one I'm in right now.* Nope! Your mission and mine is in the vocation you and I now live in. This is the place where God calls us to thrive, particularly if we are living in a sacramental vocation. God will continue to give us the grace to live out our primary vocation.

Recent studies show that 50 percent of first marriages end, second marriages end at the same clip, and only 40 percent of couples in the marriages that do last report they are happy. Our marriages can become mundane; family life can seem tedious. A priest's life can, too. But there is a certain rhythm to the life God calls us to. Not tedium, but rhythm. Marriage and family life have a rhythm that God uses to teach us to live for and with him. If we look at our vocation as though we are "trapped," or if we believe that the rhythm "steals our joy," we need to ask God to give us renewed vigor for our wife and kids.

Grace is abundant in our greatest times of need. We become saints at home. We become saints when we place our wife first, loving her as Jesus calls us to do. We become saints when we pray with her, as well. We become saints when we hold a crying baby in the middle of the night, sit at a soccer game in the cold rain, or pay for leg braces for our young child. We become saints by engaging in our kids' lives, being an intentional and present father. Not perfect, but present.

There was a time in my life when my heart said I loved my family, but my calendar said otherwise. My vocation called me to be better. It took some time, but when I began to live in "right order," my life, although busy and mundane, began to have purpose. I began to have more peace. And I began to come alive again, seeing my vocation as a mission, an adventure! I'm encouraged when I see men striving to become the husbands and fathers that God called them to be. If there is one thing St. Paul teaches us, it is to be all in in what we do. Our vocation is the place where we do this.

Lastly, we live out our mission in our secondary vocation, our work. St. Paul's secondary vocation was tent making. When Paul spent time in Corinth, he made tents to pay his way. Scripture says, "And, because he practiced the same trade, [he] stayed with them and worked, for they were tent-makers by trade" (Acts 18:3). The great apostle had a trade. Maybe it was fun for him, maybe not so much; nevertheless, he made tents to support himself. We are called to be saints in our work, too. And we sanctify our work by doing it with a purpose and mission.

You can be a builder, nurse, doctor, lawyer, landscaper, teacher, preacher, waiter, pilot, tech support, custodian, or whatever it may be. It's here, in our own form of tent making, where we find a sense of mission. Certainly, work may not be as much fun as a hobby we enjoy, and it may sometimes be hard, but it's also made holy when we offer it up to God. We all have unique gifts, and when we use them in our work, we bring God glory. We become saints by providing for our families and tithing to help those in need. We become holy by the way we treat our coworkers, by the way we carry ourselves and live with virtue in our jobs. St. Paul didn't separate his work of tent making from his mission as a preacher or his mission to be God's son. He looked at those as one and the same, as the way God used him and lived in him.

Let us be tentmakers with holy grit!

AN INVITATION

I think about the Church today and ask, "Where would St. Paul fit in?" Where would he preach and work? What would he think about the Church as it is now?

The term "the Church" encompasses a lot, from its leadership down to the person in the pew. It consists of buildings as well as communities. The Church is made up of people, places, and things. Now, more than two thousand years after the Crucifixion, the Church is fragmented into numerous denominations; yet the universal Church still stands as it did in Peter's time. And although the Church has been through crusades, wars, and crises, it is still a beacon of hope to the world in need, with Jesus at the center.

Many men today avoid faith and religion because they think it's "soft." Maybe they see other men in the Church or look at its leadership and think, *They need to be bolder* or *They could do better.* Men avoid faith for other reasons as well. I talk to lots of men who tell me the Church isn't relevant, it's boring, it's got human scandal, it's too strict, it's not strict enough, and the list goes on.

I find these excuses interesting because when men see a need, they find solutions. Most of my excuses in life stem from some internal issue. I avoid changing or owning up to something by making an excuse. Of course, some excuses are valid, but situations still require solutions. If I get a flat tire, I can choose to fix it and get to work late or I can sit on the side of the road and play the victim. Men with grit find solutions, offer alternatives that help make change for the better.

Our ability to problem solve is part gift and part curse. We can point out a problem (broken toilet) and figure out how to fix it (or get it fixed). Or we can point out a problem and walk away, saying "Not my concern." Men are world changers when we are determined to fix problems; but the adverse can be true—we can create problems. Our pride and ego can create war and division, or our courage and love can bring peace.

The Church will always stand, led by Jesus; however, human beings are imperfect, and he entrusted imperfect people to help steer it. That's not just others, but you and me. We are called to help lead the Church. We can do this by leading our families in the faith and getting involved in our local parishes and church organizations. We can do this by being men of prayer, growing each day spiritually to become God's servants first.

St. Paul was a man who pointed out problems, but then took the time to help solve them. He worked hard to bring unity to the Church and to preach truth in areas where people had gone astray. He worked at solving complex issues so that good things could come to be. He was stoned, jailed, and beaten for the sake of solving problems. Like Paul, we can either be missionaries who are part of the solution, or we can choose to complain and do nothing. We can become innovators when we see a need, or we can sit back and leave it to others.

We need more men like St. Paul in our world. Not just the preacher Paul or the tentmaker Paul. We need men who are bold and brave like Paul. Men who are willing to stand for Jesus and his truth. Men whose compassion for others leads to action. Men who don't look around and wait for others to take the lead, but who take initiative, innovate, problem solve. We need men who are willing to help the Church rather than hurt it or stand by and criticize it. We need men who will use their gifts and talents to make the world better and holier.

In 2005, Hurricane Katrina hit the Gulf Coast and caused massive casualties and damage. Many of us who lived in South Louisiana and Mississippi at the time worked in the recovery efforts following the devastation. Initially, local governments, agencies, and churches were not set up to help. There was no power and therefore no phones or internet. Time was not on anyone's side as many people were in immediate danger. If our community had waited for other people to act, those most in need would have been ignored at a critical time.

On the first night following the storm, I approached an unloading zone outside a college gym that I had heard was being used as a drop-off point for those being rescued. The people had no food, no clothes, nothing to their name. I glanced over in the dark (no power) and saw a group of men in the back of a trailer with no shirts or shoes on. They were cooking. At first, I was taken aback by their lack of clothing. I started talking with one of the men, who said, "People showed up from the flooding in the back of trucks totally naked, nothing to wear, so me and my guys gave them our clothes." He added, "We gathered all the food in our pantries, put it in the back of our trucks and trailers, and came over here and started cooking." This is what men do; they become problem solvers and innovators when there is a need.

Our cities, our neighborhoods, our churches, and our families are in desperate need of hope. We need God. You and I are called to become part of the solution in our world. If we sit back and point out the problems and don't jump in to be part of the solution, then what?

Let us become world changers, tentmakers, lovers of our families and neighbors. St. Paul's encouraging words urge us to forge ahead: "I have competed well; I have finished the race, I have kept the faith" (2 Tm 4:7).

ACTION PLAN

Take some time this week to meditate on these passages from St. Paul.

> But God proves his love for us in that while we were still sinners Christ died for us.
> —Romans 5:8

> Whatever you do, do from the heart, as for the Lord and not for others, knowing that you will receive from the Lord the due payment of the inheritance; be slaves of the Lord Christ.
> —Colossians 3:23–24

> So whoever is in Christ is a new creation: the old things have passed away; behold, new things have come.
> —2 Corinthians 5:17

> I have the strength for everything through him who empowers me.
> —Philippians 4:13

> Have no anxiety at all, but in everything, by prayer and petition, with thanksgiving, make your requests known to God. Then the peace of God that surpasses all understanding will guard your hearts and minds in Christ Jesus.
> —Philippians 4:6–7

Prayer to St. Paul

O glorious St. Paul, who from a persecutor of Christianity, didst become a most ardent apostle of zeal; and who to make known the Savior Jesus Christ unto the ends of the world didst suffer with joy imprisonment, scourgings, stonings, shipwrecks, and persecutions of every kind, and in the end didst shed thy blood to the last drop, obtain for us the grace to receive, as favors of the divine mercy, infirmities, tribulations, and misfortunes of the present life, so that the vicissitudes of this our exile will not render us cold in the service of God, but will render us always more faithful and more fervent.

V. Pray for us, St. Paul the Apostle,

R. That we may be made worthy of the promises of Christ. Amen.

Let us pray:

O God, who hast taught the multitude of the Gentiles by the preaching of blessed Paul the Apostle: grant unto us, we beseech thee, that we who keep his memory sacred, may feel the might of his intercession before thee. Through Christ our Lord. Amen.

(Taken from *The Raccolta: A Manual of Indulgences . . . Issued by the Sacred Penitentiary Apostolic* [New York: Benziger Brothers, 1957])

DISCUSSION/JOURNALING QUESTIONS

1. How is God creating in you new life, a new heart? How does he want you to see more clearly?

2. How is God inviting you to live out your primary vocation?

3. How is God inviting you to sanctify your work?

4. What problems do you see in the Church or your local community where God is inviting you to be a part of the solution?

5. How does the life of St. Paul challenge you to live your life differently?

9

LIVING WITH GRACE

Embracing a life of loving sacrifice with St. Louis Martin

It's difficult to write about Louis Martin without mentioning his wife, Marie-Azélie. They lived out their sacramental vocation together with exceptional grace, and with God at the center. I, too, hope that one day people will speak of me and my wife in the same breath, as though through our marriage we were one, in union with God and each other. That's the goal for all of us who are married. These saints, Louis and Zélie, are a model of marriage partnership.

Louis Martin was born in 1883 into a military home in Bordeaux, France. His father, a seasoned soldier, raised his children to be tough and faithful. Louis was the middle child of five; all of his siblings died before the age of thirty (Louis lived till he was seventy-one). Louis aspired to join the military, but his desire to serve God led him to discern religious life. Louis attempted to learn Latin so that he could enter a religious community as a monk. God apparently had other plans for Louis, though, as he was denied entry into the monastery.

Although disappointed, Louis was unfazed by his rejection. He was a man of holy grit, not one to give up. He became a skilled watchmaker, eventually opening his own successful business. Louis remained faithful, frequented the sacraments, and prayed daily. He grew in holiness even as he lived in the secular world. Louis was trusted in his work, respected in the community, and valued as a faith-filled friend by many who knew him.

When I look at Louis's life, I see a man to whom we can all relate. Like Louis, we are men who are called each day to wake up with a purpose. We are called to work, provide, and yet remain faithful in the world and culture in which we live. We are men who are moved to rise up, to live above the fray, to allow faith, love, and hope to lead the way. We are men who are called to live joyfully and virtuously, men who are called to prayer, sacraments, and parish life. Louis did these things simply and faithfully. Louis lived this way daily.

Louis's life as a single man was extraordinary and a powerful example to the single. He lived out his day-to-day life with grace—working, praying, and playing, all while giving glory to God. I often tell young men who are discerning their vocation, "Become the person you are looking for. Don't worry so much about finding the right person as much as becoming the person you want to be; become the person someone is looking for." Be that man!

Louis's intention was to strive to be "that man," the man God was calling him to be, never thinking marriage was on the horizon. The vocation to marriage, however, didn't take second place to religious life in God's eyes. No. God's plan all along was for Louis to be a husband and father. God's design for Louis was to be holy at home with his family. And as God parted the Red Sea for the Israelites, so would he make a way for Louis to meet his bride.

His future wife, Zélie, was a holy woman, discerning religious life while working as a successful lace maker. She was running her own lace-making business (impressive, especially during the mid-1800s) when she crossed paths with Louis on the Saint-Léonard Bridge in Alençon, France. Struck by Louis's dignified demeanor and noble face, Zélie heard an interior voice say, "This is he whom I have prepared for you." God had brought them together, and they would marry three months later. The sea parted, and they walked through it.

As I mentioned earlier, my life revolved around sports as I was growing up. While playing ball in college, I was also in the process of a deeper conversion. My faith was taking root, little by little. After many failed attempts to find true love, I surrendered my vocation to the Lord. I felt a tug to make God the center of my life and began to grow closer to him. Many would assume I was being called to become a priest or a religious. But holy grit isn't meant just for those in religious life; it's for everyone. It's for me and you. Holiness was for Louis Martin too, despite his failed attempt to become a monk. He didn't give up striving for holiness. As a matter of fact, he did the opposite.

While I was wrestling with discerning my vocation, a spiritual mentor posed a simple question that I hadn't thought about. He asked, "Which vocation will challenge you or call you to holiness the most?" I had never considered this question. As I prayed about it, it became clear in my heart that marriage would call me to holiness the most. It would challenge me to become the man I could not become on my own. That's what a sacrament does. A sacrament is God's presence active in our life. A sacrament is an invisible sign of God's physical reality, his life in us. A sacrament activates grace (God) in our life. The Holy Spirit begins to move in us. When we give God permission to move in our life, grace abounds, flows, and moves us downstream.

I had no idea of any of this at the time I got married. Now, twenty-five years later, I get it. My vocation and yours is the avenue toward greater love, holiness, and pursuit of God. We don't do this on our own, but with God. Our vocation is the way we grow in holiness, through grace. Like Louis, I met my future wife when I was not looking for her, but during a time when I had surrendered, let go, and allowed God's grace to flow and to take charge of my life.

Louis Martin said about his marriage, "Soon we'll have the intimate happiness of the family, and it's this beauty that brings us closer to him." Your vocation is the springboard toward the life God has created for you. It is here, in the daily grind, that you and I become men of holy grit!

It is written about Louis and Zélie, "They did not see their marriage as a normal arrangement between two middle-class families of Alençon, but as a total opening to the will of God." The couple decided that God would always be "the first served" in their marriage. On July 13, 1858, at the Basilica of Notre-Dame d'Alençon, Louis and Zélie stood before God, the altar of sacrifice, each other, and friends to declare their sacramental vows to each other. They remained faithful to each other in good times and bad, in sickness and in health. Their family grew, and their children brought joy into their lives. They had nine kids, five of whom survived infancy. All five of their daughters entered religious life.

In 1876, Zélie passed away. After eighteen years of a loving marriage and at the end of a hard-fought battle with cancer, her journey to heaven was complete. With five daughters to raise, Louis moved to Lisieux to be closer to family. He remained faithful as a man of God and a father until his death in 1894. He died knowing that his children were on the path toward heaven.

Louis and Zélie are well known as the parents of St. Thérèse of Lisieux, one of the most popular saints of our time. A spiritual warrior, writer, and doctor of the Church, St. Thérèse would credit her family for her love of God. She said, "The good God gave me a father and a mother more worthy of heaven than of earth." The love she saw in her parents showed her how God loves. St. Thérèse's impact on the world and in the Church remains evident today.

On October 18, 2015, Louis and Zélie became the first spouses in the Church's history to be canonized as a couple. The two who became one flesh, united in Jesus in Holy Matrimony, would enter into sainthood together. The liturgical feast of St. Louis Martin and St. Marie-Azélie Guérin is celebrated on July 12.

EMBRACING OUR ROLE

St. Louis Martin was a man who embraced his role as a husband, father, friend, and provider. He had no exit plan; he was all in on what God put before him. His life challenges me to become "that man," too. St. Louis challenges me to be all in.

I often have conversations with men who wrestle with their state in life. The daily rhythms of life have become mundane or tedious, and they sometimes view their vocation as more of a burden than a gift. A priest who is bitter, tired, apathetic, and unmotivated is sad to see. A husband and father who has distanced himself from his role, settling for mediocrity in loving his wife and children, is sad to see as well. A single man who lacks joy in his state of life, struggling to become who God made him to be, is also sad to see.

This is certainly not to discount how difficult it can be to live out our call. We all know it is hard! The seasons of life we experience in our vocation can at times seem overwhelming. This is why our vocation calls us to be gritty *and* holy, not one without the other. And this is why so many men give up or give in.

God doesn't call us to a vocation that's easy. He also doesn't call us to a vocation that lacks joy and love. But achieving these things takes work. Our effort says more about us than the outcome. The scoreboard of life doesn't matter as much as the effort on the field. Our field of play is the one we live in every day, our homes. There are days when my state of life is extremely joyful, and there are days when it is extremely hard, my tank feels empty. Only God can fill our tanks. And when we lean totally on him, by his grace we become whole again.

We are all called to embrace our role, to own it, to wear it as though it is part of us, because it is who we are. And it's when we embrace our vocation that we begin to thrive in it. When we embrace our state of life, we begin to work at it and put effort into it. Embracing is the first step to moving forward in the work God calls us to. God has more in store for us, abundant life. This abundance is found in a relationship with Jesus, lived out in our vocation.

The Vatican II document *Lumen Gentium* (*Light of the Nations*) says this about how we live out our vocations as lay, married people: "They live in the world, that is, in each and in all of the secular professions and occupations. They live in the ordinary circumstances of family and social life, from which the very web of their existence is woven. They are called there by God that by exercising their proper function and led by the spirit of the Gospel they may work for the sanctification of the world from within as a leaven" (para. 31). It is in the ordinary that we become extraordinary men, holy and gritty.

When Gretchen and I were going through marriage preparation, we met with the priest who was going to marry us. He just happened to be a bishop, Bishop Sam Jacobs. He had been my mentor and friend for years, and he became friends with us as a couple, too. He was never short on challenging me to be holy and gritty. He knew I needed to be challenged. I liked being challenged. I'd rather be told the hard truth than some watered-down version that makes me feel good. Bishop Jacobs was a big influence in helping me keep the train on the tracks.

In one of our engagement meetings, the bishop said to me, "Your main role as a husband is to get Gretchen to heaven." It took me a moment to grasp what he was saying. I thought he would say my main role was to make money, to provide for our family, or to make her happy. Nope. My main job is to get my wife to heaven! "What's the alternative?" I asked him. To which he replied, "There is no exit strategy." It's heaven or bust!

Gulp!

This is what Louis Martin did with great intention. He embraced his role, knowing that it extended well beyond being a watchmaker. To water down the role of a husband and father to simply being a provider is silly. To water down the role of a priest to simply being a decision maker or sacrament provider is naive. We are made for more. We men are missionaries who are called to live in the mission of our own homes, helping those who live there to find Jesus and get to heaven. Priests are referred to as fathers for a reason, because they are called to help the families assigned to their care to get to heaven. St. Louis went to his deathbed knowing that his children were on the path to heaven, that his wife Zélie was there, and that when he was laid to rest, he would hear the words of Jesus, "Well done, my good and faithful servant" (Mt 25:23).

I had to embrace my role as husband and father before I could help get my wife and kids to heaven. I had to get myself on that path first. For as Jesus says, "Can a blind person guide a blind person? Will not both fall into a pit?" (Lk 6:39). I had to begin to see before I could lead my wife and family. The wonderful thing about the vocation of marriage is that husbands and wives help each other to see. We become God's mercy, love, and healing for the other person, so they can see better. I see more clearly because of my wife and children.

I also had to acknowledge that there is no exit plan. I'm all in. To help get my wife to heaven is not easy, and I'm certainly not the best at it, but I'm all in. St. Louis Martin was all in, too. He had no back door to walk out of when things got hard. Instead of dreaming of the monastery when his house was noisy, he took time to pray. He even built a prayer space in his attic where he could spend time contemplating. His children loved to go to that space and pray, too. Like father, like children. You see this often in the home, kids modeling their dads, for good or bad. You see this too in churches, parishioners modeling their priest.

St. Louis's calling was right in front of him in the faces of his wife, Zélie, and his five living daughters. This family was his vocation.

In his opening address to the Thirteenth Synod of Bishops on the New Evangelization in 2012, Pope Benedict said in regard to living a holy marriage: "Matrimony is a Gospel in itself, a Good News for the world of today, especially the deChristianized world. The union of a man and a woman, their becoming 'one flesh' in charity, in fruitful and indissoluble love, is a sign that speaks of God with a force and an eloquence." St. Louis Martin lived his vocation with "force and eloquence," modeling for us what it means to be a man of holy grit.

AN INVITATION

Over the years in my work as a consultant, one of the things I've learned from prosperous business folks is that to be successful at something, there can be no backup plan. You have to give it all you have. Years ago, I spent some time with an NFL team. As I got to know the men on the team, I asked them questions about how they achieved this level of success. The common thread in what these guys told me was that they were all in. "I had no other plan, this was the plan," each said.

It's one thing to go all in with our profession, and it's another thing to go all in with our vocation. Our jobs will end one day. We will get old and someone younger will take our place. We will retire or die, but it will end one way or another. Likewise, pro athletes eventually can't play any longer; their bodies give out, and they can no longer do what they once could. Our vocation, however, lasts forever. It is the gift that will cement our legacy. Our life's work is to unite our gritty masculinity with our desire to know God in the greatest task we will be asked to take on, our vocation.

Things become blurry when we don't embrace our role in our vocation. When things get hard, we start to look for the exit door. Jesus asked his disciples to go all in, and some decided to walk away. But many stayed, and the ones who did experienced abundant life even when it got hard. To be a man of holy grit, to live the life of discipleship to which we are called, takes everything we have. There is no exit door because being a disciple is not *what we do*, it's *who we are*. And we live out our calling as a disciple in and through our vocation.

The currents of the world are strong, and the undertow will pull us away from our calling as men. There are distractions, good and bad. There are opportunities and exit doors. There are temptations, wide roads to travel. St. Louis Martin said, "Do as I did: pray, and you will not be carried away by the current." He too felt the temptation to bolt when things got hard. Being a husband, provider, and father did not come easy to him, but because he had faith, it became doable.

When my wife and I had our first child, we had no idea what we were doing. I was hit with the responsibility of being a dad and a provider for another, totally helpless human. A friend reminded me that my main role as a dad was to get my daughter to heaven. That's a tall task, but I took it to heart. I still do. You can ask any of my five children about me, and they will tell you stories showing how imperfect I am. But my desire to get them to heaven is real, and I'm intentional about it. If anything, my love for God and my love for their mother are the best gifts I can give them. Any attempts at being the "perfect dad" are over; I'm not good at perfection. But I can love, despite my imperfections. I can be committed despite my shortcomings. I can seal the exit door. I can swim against the current. And with God's grace and presence, I can not only survive but thrive, most days.

Before my daughter got engaged, I met with the young man (Matt, whom I like very much) about their relationship. I told him that when Marie was born, I made a promise to God that as her father I would help get her to heaven. He nodded, "Yes, sir." Then I said, "When she marries you, that becomes your job. So if you want to marry my daughter, that's the only thing I ask, that you help her get to heaven." Months later, when he came to talk to me about getting engaged, he said, "I've been thinking about what you said about getting Marie to heaven, and that's what I want to do. I want to get her to heaven." Joy and gratitude welled up inside me, because that's all I can ask for. What I can do and what you can do is what St. Louis Martin did. Each day strive to ensure that your wife and kids, by God's loving and powerful grace, are on the path to heaven.

Louis and Zélie Martin lived an extraordinary life. Their life was extraordinary not because they did anything amazing or world changing, but because of their faith in God. They lived ordinary lives with extraordinary faith. The invitation for us as men is to look at their life, their example, and try to emulate them, to love as they did. When I consider their life's work, I'm challenged to become better, and it's a challenge I'm willing to accept because it's what will make me happy. You and I are called to be extraordinary in the ordinary, to live great lives by living our vocation to the fullest. This is where we become men of holy grit!

ACTION PLAN

1. Create an action plan for your marriage:

   Think of three things you can be more intentional about in your relationship with your wife. Write them down and begin to work on them. For example, create quality time. Schedule date nights, pray together, go on a couples' retreat, attend Mass together, and so on.

2. Create an action plan for your kids:

   Think of three things you can be more intentional about in your relationship with your children. Write them down and begin to work on them. For example, spend some time with them doing what they like. Do activities together, write them a letter, and so on.

3. Create an action plan for yourself:

   Think of three things you can be more intentional about personally that will help you be a better husband, father, priest, or single man. Write them down and begin to work on them. For example, schedule more time in Eucharistic Adoration, join a Bible study, and so on.

Prayer for the Intercession of St. Louis Martin

Jesus, Mary, and Joseph, in you we contemplate the splendor of true Love.

Through the intercession of Sts. Louis and Zélie,

we ask that our families too be places of communion and prayer,

authentic schools of the Gospel and small domestic churches.

Holy Family of Nazareth, may families never again experience violence, rejection,

or division. May all who have been hurt or scandalized find comfort and healing.

Jesus, Mary, and Joseph, to you we turn with trust; help us always be mindful of

the sacredness of marriage, family life, and its beauty in God's plan.

Sts. Louis and Zélie Martin, pray for us.

Amen.

DISCUSSION/JOURNALING QUESTIONS

1. How does the life of St. Louis and Zélie challenge you?

2. In what ways does the life of St. Louis Martin motivate you to become better?

3. What is the toughest challenge of living out your vocation?

4. How is God inviting you to grow in your faith and in your vocation?

5.   What positive changes can you make in your life that will have an impact on your vocation?

10

THE WILL TO WIN

Finishing the race with St. John Paul II

Known to many as "JP2," St. John Paul II was one of the most influential people of the twentieth century: spiritually, theologically, politically, and socially. One can argue that, other than St. Teresa of Calcutta, there is no greater saint of our time—none more courageous, bold, and faithful. JP2 was a saint who showed the world how to live. He lived life to the full, he ran the race, he finished strong—persevering heroically with Christ to the very end. He was a man of holy grit.

JP2 was born Karol Józef Wojtyła on May 18, 1920, in Wadowice, Poland, just fifteen miles from Auschwitz, the largest of the Nazi concentration camps. The threat of war in Poland was a looming fear for Karol when he was growing up. Although Poland remained independent during his childhood, that would soon change.

Karol was raised in a simple middle-class family. His father was a lieutenant in the Polish military. He was disciplined, gritty, and faithful, making sure Karol and his older brother, Edmund, practiced the Catholic faith. His mother, Emilia, died when Karol was a young boy. Karol said, "I had not yet made my First Holy Communion when I lost my mother: I was barely nine years old." Sadly, his brother would pass away four years later while serving those stricken with scarlet fever, leaving only Karol and his father.

Karol would say of his dad: "My father's words played a very important role because they directed me toward becoming a true worshiper of God." This is our aim as fathers, to be men who "direct" our families to become "true worshipers of God."

Karol grew up playing sports, participating in theater, and excelling in academics. He graduated as valedictorian of his class. He was a gritty young man who worked hard and played hard. He had lots of friends, and those close to him called him Lolek, which means "free man." Karol was free, full of life, resilient; and he was active in his school, church, and community.

After high school, he and his father moved to Kraków, where Karol attended university. Not long after he entered college, Nazi Germany invaded Poland. Karol and his father evacuated east for safety, returning soon after Russia took over. Upon their return, they found that many people had been sent away to concentration camps. Life was different; freedom and independence were lost.

Karol continued his academic studies in secret, also getting a job as a factory laborer to avoid the Nazi regime and the threat of deportation. His faith guided him. He was a blue-collar worker by day and a college student studying underground at night. Karol exemplified tenacity and a willingness to finish what he started despite extreme opposition.

When he returned home from work at the factory one evening, Karol found his father dead from a heart attack. Karol had already experienced suffering and trials; now his role model and guide was gone. Karol later described how his father's influence had affected his faith: "I was left alone with my father, a deeply religious man. Day after day I was able to observe the austere way in which he lived ... his example was in a way my first seminary, a kind of domestic seminary."

Karol was orphaned and alone before his twenty-first birthday, having lost both his parents and his older brother. He found comfort in his Catholic faith and deep devotion to the Lord. His faith in Christ was the light that showed him the path. As the psalm says, "Your word is a lamp for my feet, a light for my path" (119:105).

In occupied Poland, Karol experienced the pain and trauma of war on top of the loss of his family. These trials would sharpen his faith and strengthen his resolve to serve God. As Peter wrote to Christians under threat of persecution, "In this you rejoice, although now for a little while you may have to suffer through various trials, so that genuineness of your faith, more precious than gold that is perishable even though tested by fire, may prove to be for praise, glory, and honor at the revelation of Jesus Christ" (1 Pt 1:6–7). Karol's heart would be purified by these trials as his faith was "tested by fire."

We all experience trials in our lives. I once was told by a spiritual adviser, "With God nothing is lost, it's all for gain. God uses everything for our good." God uses all of the pain, suffering, and trials we undergo to form us for the good. God takes our mistakes, our regrets, and our past and uses those too. Nothing is lost in Christ.

St. Paul said it best: "Whatever gains I had, these I have come to consider a loss because of Christ. More than that, I even consider everything as a loss because of the supreme good of knowing Christ Jesus my Lord. For his sake I have accepted the loss of all things and I consider them so much rubbish, that I may gain Christ and be found in him" (Phil 3:7–9). St. Paul's claim is that in Christ, we gain back what was lost. Jesus takes our trials, sufferings, and heartache and makes something beautiful and good out of them.

Thus, when you and I are in the fire (trial), God uses it to make us more gritty and holy. When I look back on challenging times in my life, I can see the hand of God at work, but in the midst of the trial it is difficult to have this perspective. Just as gold goes into a furnace and comes out purified and beautiful to behold, so too do we. Nothing was lost in Karol's life; God took all of his trials and made them into "gold."

JP2 said, "I plead with you—never, ever give up on hope, never doubt, never tire, and never become discouraged." One of the major themes of his life was hope. JP2 was a beacon of hope to the world because of his steadfast hope in Jesus. Karol's hope sprang from his deep faith, even as he endured suffering and trials. He saw light in the darkness. Despite war, he had hope. Despite losing his family, he had hope. He lived out the scripture that says, "Let us hold unwaveringly to our confession that gives us hope, for he who made the promise is trustworthy" (Heb 10:23).

On days when life seems overwhelming, things can look hopeless. But hope is not something that disappears; it's always there. Because Jesus is hope. And in the midst of trials, darkness, good and bad days, he is present. Hope is the foundation of our life; without it we lose sight, darkness overcomes us, and we can't see the race we are running. The finish line seems too far. The race of life begins with knowing that there is a finish line, and that no matter how hard the race is, we can get there. That is hope.

The trials that Karol endured only prepared him more for what God was asking of him, which was a lot. The trials we endure are preparing us, too, for what God has in store. Our strength comes from God alone, and he builds our spiritual fortitude through trials.

As a young man, Karol entered the seminary to study to become a priest. He resolved to do what God asked of him, no matter what. His studies were interrupted when the Nazis invaded Poland, but eventually he enrolled in an underground seminary, dressing as a cleric to avoid detection by the Nazis. Karol Józef Wojtyła was ordained to the priesthood in November of 1946 at the age of twenty-six.

Fr. Wojtyła found true happiness in his vocation as a priest. He went on to finish his doctoral studies in Rome and eventually was assigned as associate pastor of a church in his home country of Poland. It was here, back home, as a young priest that he began to bring Christ to those in need. He started working with youth, young adults, and married couples. He went camping, hiked, and said Mass on outdoor adventures with those who were with him. He was not afraid, despite Poland's political turmoil. He learned to have a father's heart, from his own father and from deep prayer with God, letting himself be loved by God the Father. It was as a simple priest that his fatherly heart grew to love his flock. His fatherly heart would guide him throughout his life in his priestly ministry.

In 1958, Fr. Wojtyła was named auxiliary bishop, and five years later he was named archbishop of Kraków. In 1967, he was named to the College of Cardinals. In 1978, John Paul I was elected pope. After thirty-three days in the papacy, he died suddenly, thus causing the College of Cardinals to reconvene. Surprisingly, they voted to elect Karol Wojtyła as pope.

Cardinal Wojtyła became pope on October 16, 1978, and took the name John Paul II because of his deep devotion to St. John of the Cross and his respect for his predecessor, John Paul I. He was the 263rd successor to Peter and the first non-Italian pope in 455 years. John Paul II was to have one of the longest pontificates in the history of the Church, lasting nearly twenty-seven years. He retained his episcopal motto, drawn from St. Louis de Montfort, *"Totus Tuus—*totally yours." *Totus Tuus* was a way of life for JP2. He lived with total abandon and surrender to God. His papacy was legendary, and he left a legacy of faith for generations to come.

On April 2, 2005, the world kept solemn vigil as Pope John Paul II, who suffered with Christ in his long battle with Parkinson's disease, succumbed at the age of eighty-four. His last words were a profound expression of his faith and love for God: "Let me go to my Father's house." He longed to be with Jesus, and his time had finally come.

Pope John Paul II passed away on Divine Mercy Sunday. For a generation he was "the pope," the Vicar of Christ. He made an impact on millions, myself included. He brought hope to individuals and to the Church. He breathed new life into our world as he helped build bridges and knock down barriers. In many ways, he was a hero, a gritty and holy man from Poland who God used to do tremendous things. In 2014, he was canonized St. John Paul II as millions looked on and celebrated.

JP2 said as he got older, "Death itself is anything but an event without hope. It is the door which opens wide on eternity and, for those who live in Christ, an experience of participation in the mystery of his Death and Resurrection." St. John Paul II was a man of holy grit, a man who showed us how to finish strong, how to love Christ to the end and meet him face-to-face in eternity—how to have hope. At his funeral, his friend Pope Benedict XVI said, "We can be sure that our beloved Pope is standing today at the window of the Father's house, that he sees us and blesses us."

FINISHING STRONG

"Be not afraid!" These were the first words of Pope John Paul II in his inaugural address in 1978. As a young adult, I encountered JP2 in Denver in 1993, and my vision of how to be a man changed forever. I was in the crowd at World Youth Day when this man with holy grit said, from the depths of his heart, "Be not afraid, open wide the doors of Christ."

When I encountered the pope that day in Colorado, I was a wandering young man who needed a father's spiritual voice to help me move forward. "Be not afraid" were the words I needed to hear. I desired to have courage and to live my life for Christ, to be free from the weight of the world and the guilt of my sinful past. JP2 said, "The worst prison would be a closed heart." I wanted to be set free from the prison of my own heart and the fears that threw away the key to unlock it.

Most of us have heard the term "finish strong." It's something we say to motivate someone to give it their all. This is nothing new; St. Paul refers to it in scripture when he speaks of finishing the race (see 2 Timothy 4:7). There are three parts to the race of life: the start, the trek itself, and the finish line. We all have different starting points in our spiritual journeys, we all have unique timelines, and we all end at the finish line at our own pace. But what we all have in common is a start, the trek itself, and a finish. JP2 lived the race of life with total trust and abandonment. He lived with his eyes on the eternal prize, yet he enjoyed the trek along the way, and he crossed the finish line with grit.

When I encountered JP2 in 1993, he had survived two attempts on his life. Once he was shot, another time he was stabbed. On May 13, 1981, the pope was shot four times in an attempted assassination by Mehmet Ali Ağca in St. Peter's Square. The doctors who treated JP2 after the attack said there was no way he should have survived the gunshot wounds. He would say of the shooting, "In everything that happened to me on that day, I felt [the Mother of God's] extraordinary motherly protection and care, which turned out to be stronger than the deadly bullet." God protected him, as did the Blessed Mother.

JP2's faith moved him to great compassion for his attacker. When the world said revenge, the pope offered mercy. The strength to survive a shooting is one thing, but the courage to visit your attacker in prison, offering him forgiveness, is another. That's what JP2 did. He had a powerful face-to-face meeting with Mehmet Ali Ağca, where he forgave his attacker and heard his confession.

Now JP2 added *mercy* to his papal themes of *hope* and *courage*. He taught the world to forgive as Jesus does. In 1982, almost a year to the day after the assassination attempt by Mehmet Ali Ağca, the pope was stabbed by a radical priest while saying Mass in Fatima, Portugal. The pope finished saying Mass while bleeding under his vestments, not knowing the depth of the knife wound until he undressed. He again would have the courage to forgive his attacker, to love his enemy.

I think about my life and wonder if I would have had the same courage as JP2 when faced with attempts to kill me. I long to have the love and mercy he had. I'm inspired by his life, words, and actions. He lived what he preached. JP2 said, "You, too, be courageous! The world needs convinced and fearless witnesses. It is not enough to discuss, it is necessary to act." It is not enough to just be gritty. No. The challenge for us men is to seek to be saints, gritty ones, yes, but also holy ones!

When I arrived in Denver with my youth group, my intentions were for fun and mischief more than prayer. But I was searching and God's grace moved, despite my attitude. I was mesmerized and intrigued by JP2. At that point in my life I was looking for an example of a man with grit and godliness, and I found him on World Youth Day. Despite the attacks on his life, the pope rode around in a vehicle with no bulletproof casing. He came close to the crowd of over a million people without concern for his life, similar to the way Christ walked through the streets when he knew the Pharisees were out to capture him. JP2 came close to us, as Jesus did with the woman at the well, the woman caught in adultery, Lazarus in the grave. Jesus was not afraid to be near the mess, to "smell like his sheep," his flock.

As I leaned up against the barrier along the path, Pope John Paul II locked eyes with me. He touched my hand. He blessed me. I saw hope. I saw courage. I saw love. I saw mercy. I saw Jesus in him, and at that moment, I realized that grittiness and holiness could coexist—that my life could be both godly and courageous.

JP2 said, "It is Jesus who stirs in you the desire to do something great with your lives, the will to follow an ideal, the refusal to allow yourselves to be ground down by mediocrity, the courage to commit yourselves humbly and patiently to improving yourselves and society, making the world more human and more fraternal." These words are what you and I are created for, to live with purpose and to have a mission.

God invites us to join him in this mission, like JP2, to bring hope, love, and courage to a world in need. Men are made for greatness—to be leaders, to guide our families, our friends, our cities, and our churches. We are made to serve, give, and guide. We are created to protect, defend, and build God's kingdom. We are made for grit, created for holiness.

AN INVITATION

There was a point in my spiritual journey when I realized that what God had done in my heart could not be separated or compartmentalized. The parts of my divided heart had to merge as one. My life is all of me, spiritual, physical, and emotional. All of me belongs to God. It *must* belong to him, or my life will fall apart. I'm certain that you, too, have come to a point in your journey where you realize there is more to life than what the world offers. I'm certain that you are ready to integrate your total self, your whole life, with the life of Jesus. Why? Because you and I are created for this purpose.

St. John Paul II lived during a time in history when men needed a model of manliness to follow. He lived heroically, courageously, and lovingly. His life was gritty *and* holy. JP2 shows us that the life God calls us to live is possible. God can take us and make something great. Our mission as men is to allow God to integrate and incorporate all of him with all of ourselves.

I am coming to the realization that I can live with the motto of St. John Paul II, "Be not afraid," and each day I can, with Christ, "finish strong," like he did. My life changed the day I encountered this amazing saint. Although brief, that moment showed me a real man living out the real Gospel. And I knew that what my heart desired was possible. It wasn't a total or sudden change, but a new conversion began to take hold in me. JP2 showed me that I, too, could live with an open heart, abandoning my life to God. I no longer had to be a prisoner in my own heart, closed off from God and others. You and I are created for love, and to love.

This was another central theme in St. John Paul II's life, *love*. We are all created out of God's love, and we are created to receive and give his love. Love transforms us, it transforms others, and it transforms the world. JP2 said, "Do not forget that true love sets no conditions. It does not calculate or complain, but simply loves." Jesus gave himself totally for us, holding nothing back. This is how God loves us and in return we love others. Men are created to model the love of Christ in our families, in our friendships, and in our world. We are made whole when we mesh our life with the life of Christ.

Our lives have tremendous meaning, but time is short. Our brief trek on this earth is but a blip on a screen. We have a short time to live life fully and to make an impact on the world. Our trek is our time to shine for Christ and to bring glory to God each and every day. St. John Paul II said, "The future starts today, not tomorrow." Our trek starts now, and then again tomorrow, until we finish strong at the end.

Our mission is in front of us each day. We can't bury our heads in the sand or move into a bunker to escape the world. No, we are called to live abundantly and courageously in the world. JP2 said, "True holiness does not mean a flight from the world; rather, it lies in the effort to incarnate the Gospel in everyday life, in the family, at school, and at work, and in social and political involvement." This is our calling.

We are all called to be men of holy grit. Men on a mission, living with a purpose, with God at the core. As St. John Paul II liked to say, quoting St. Catherine of Siena, "Become who you were meant to be and you will set the world on fire." We are meant to be men of godliness and courage. Men who set the world on fire. Imagine a world where we live this out, together! Men of holy grit!

ACTION PLAN

1. Read the quote from JP2 below, taken from his twelfth World Youth Day address. Take some time to come up with a plan to make prayer a central part of your life. What is your plan each day, each week, to grow your prayer life with Jesus?

    Remember that you are never alone, Christ is with you on your journey every day of your lives! He has called you and chosen you to live in the freedom of the children of God. Turn to him in prayer and in love. Ask him to grant you the courage and strength to live in this freedom always.

2. Read the text from St. John Paul II below. How is Jesus inviting you to live for him daily, on mission? Take some time to reflect and journal about how God is inviting you to do his work each day.

> Walk with him who is "the Way, the Truth and the Life"! The most beautiful and stirring adventure that can happen to you is the personal meeting with Jesus, who is the only one who gives real meaning to our lives.

3. JP2 lived his life totally abandoned to the love of God. Read the quote below. What is your action plan for growing deeper in love with Jesus as you move forward each day?

> Today Christ is asking each of you the same question: do you love me? He is not asking you whether you know how to speak to crowds, whether you can direct an organization or manage an estate. He is asking you to love him. All the rest will ensue.

Prayer to St. John Paul II

Oh, St. John Paul, from the window of heaven, grant us your blessing! Bless the Church that you loved and served and guided, courageously leading her along the paths of the world in order to bring Jesus to everyone and everyone to Jesus. Bless the young, who were your great passion. Help them dream again, help them look up to the heavens again to find the light that illuminates the paths of life here on earth.

May you bless each and every family! You warned of Satan's assault against this precious and indispensable divine spark that God lit on earth. St. John Paul, with your prayer, may you protect the family and every life that blossoms from the family.

Pray for the whole world, which is still marked by tensions, wars, and injustice. You opposed war by invoking dialogue and planting the seeds of love: pray for us so that we may be tireless sowers of peace.

Oh, St. John Paul, from heaven's window, where we see you beside Mary, send God's blessing down upon us all. Amen.

DISCUSSION/JOURNALING QUESTIONS

1. Courage is one of the main themes in the life of JP2. How is God calling you to be more courageous, more trusting, in your life?

2. Love is another important theme in the life of JP2. How is God calling you to deepen your understanding of love, for yourself and for others?

3. Forgiveness and mercy are themes in the life of JP2. In what ways is God calling you to incorporate these virtues into your life?

4. Faith is a central theme in the life of JP2. How is God inviting you to increase your faith in him?

5. Hope is a powerful theme in the life of JP2. How is God inviting you to grow in the virtue of hope?

EPILOGUE

In an effort to be completely transparent, after writing this book I decided to add this epilogue. I wanted to share with you what happened to me, and to my soul, as I sat down over the course of months to put this book together.

When I began writing, I had two goals in mind. First, I wanted to write about a subject I was genuinely passionate about. I did not want to take on a project unless it was something I felt I could put my heart into and believe in. Second, I wanted to write for an audience I connected with and believed in. Men. As a man, I know the struggles of living a manly existence. It is one I deal with daily. I'm no expert, but I'm a gritty guy, like you, grinding it out on my journey.

I achieved those two goals, but what I wasn't prepared for was the impact this book would have on me personally. The saints I encountered, studied, and learned about while writing this book have had an influence on me that I did not expect. Something happened to me as I connected with these saints.

You see, I never really connected with saints. I was baptized Catholic as a kid, but I did not practice my faith well or know much about it. I fell away. I wandered. And when I had my "reversion" to the faith as a young man, I didn't know much about the Church, its beliefs, or its theology. To me, saints were people who lived good and godly lives, but they didn't affect my own story. They were dead, literally, and therefore were a part of history.

Over the years I began to learn more about the Church and its theology, but the saints were still in the past, historic. I took an academic approach to learning about them, thinking we can benefit from reading about them but not "live life" with them.

Then, a few years back, my wife and I were going through a time of major decisions in our life: in our family, our careers, schools for our children, location changes, and other life transitions. We were living in a massive state of discernment that continued for a year. On one occasion my spiritual director, Fr. Bob, suggested that we call in an army, a community of folks to help us discern. "Family? Friends?" I asked. He said, "No, an army, a community of saints." *Huh?*

So in faith we prayed about it and picked six saints to join us in our intense time of discernment. We asked St. Joan of Arc, the Blessed Virgin Mary, St. Joseph, St. Paul, St. Peter, and St. John Paul II to help us discern. "This is all a formality," I thought.

Nope. As we invited these saints to pray along with us, miracles began to happen, both in our hearts and in our discernment. We personally began to experience saints who were real, alive. And doors began to open and close in our discernment, dominoes fell into place miraculously. God was moving, and our community of saints propelled us forward, cheering us on. They carried us through, supporting us along the way. During this process my heart began to open up, and I started to see the saints not only as holy people who have gone before me but as people who are alive today.

A canonized saint is someone who is acknowledged by the Church as having lived a holy life, who is alive in heaven, and who continues to intercede and participate in the life of God. All saints have had miracles attributed to them, meaning they are living and active. The letter to the Hebrews encourages us, "Therefore, since we are surrounded by so great a cloud of witnesses, let us rid ourselves of every burden and sin that clings to us and persevere in running the race that lies before us while keeping our eyes fixed on Jesus, the leader and perfecter of faith" (12:1–2). The "cloud of witnesses" who surround us are the saints. They are the community of believers who have gone before us yet who live life with us each day.

Much of the time I spent on this project was not in the writing; it was in praying to discern which saints, out of the thousands the Church has canonized, would be the focus of the ten chapters. It wasn't easy to choose. I was consumed with researching each saint, learning about them, and trying to connect with them personally, emotionally, and spiritually. And an amazing thing happened. I began to experience a real-life relationship with each one of these holy men. I was challenged by their lives, my heart was united with them on this journey, and I also felt their intercession, their presence with me. It was like we built a friendship, a heavenly one.

What happened? Reflecting on St. Joseph's radical yes to God's will has opened my heart to more fervently seek God's will for my life. St. Augustine came alive to me, teaching me how to overcome obstacles and strive more fully for true happiness in Christ. St. Thomas More taught me to have courage in the public square, and he gave me a new awakening to being a dad. St. Ignatius walked with me, showing me how to pray better and how to love Jesus in prayer. Padre Pio is teaching me faith and especially trust, which is one of my greatest needs. St. Peter gave me a new heart for Confession and for proclaiming Jesus as Lord of my life. St. Maximilian Kolbe has taught me to love my neighbor and to be more sacrificial in my love, something I've always wanted. St. Paul has encouraged me to not give up, to continue to run the race of life no matter the shipwrecks along the way. St. Louis Martin radically shifted my heart to fall in love with my wife and children again. I still feel him with me. And St. John Paul II knew that my heart needs hope, daily, and I feel a new outpouring of hope in my life.

I hope this book does more for you than offer information about some interesting saints. It is a book that invites you into a living relationship with Jesus and the saints. Get an army, a committee to join you. Learn and pray with these amazing men who have gone before us and who accompany us in our daily life. Be refreshed, renewed, and allow your heart to be transformed, as mine continues to be. Let's become more like them, holy and gritty!

Paul George is a Catholic speaker, teacher, and author of several books, including *Rethink Happiness*. He is the cofounder of Adore Ministries and served as its president for eight years. He has more than twenty-five years of ministry experience on the parish, diocesan, and national levels.

George is a consultant and speaker and, through his organization The Art of Living, serves churches, schools, organizations, and corporations throughout the world with their strategies, values, and missions. George is the host of a national radio show and podcast, *The Paul George Show*. He is a speaker at Steubenville conferences and spoke at World Youth Day in both Rome and Australia.

George earned his bachelor's degree from Louisiana College in 1997 and his master's degree in theological studies from the University of Dallas in 2008. He is a former college baseball and football player. George has served as national director of Life Teen International and a professor of theology at the Aquinas Institute. He wrote several Bible studies, including *The Art of Living*, *Let's Be Honest*, and *What If*. He also authored both a student's guide and a teacher's guide to the new YOUCAT.

Paul and his wife, Gretchen, live in Lafayette, Louisiana, with their five children.

www.discovertheartofliving.com

Twitter, Instagram: @paulgeorgeii

ALSO BY
PAUL GEORGE

Rethink Happiness
Dare to Embrace God and Experience True Joy

For the past twenty years Paul George has helped
fellow Catholics discover their purpose by searching themselves,
reorganizing their priorities, and establishing a personal relationship
with Jesus Christ. In *Rethink Happiness*, George invites you to pursue
authentic happiness by surrendering your life to God
and focusing on simple joys: daily prayer, a minimalist lifestyle,
meaningful relationships, and an ongoing pursuit of God's will.

Embedded in Catholic wisdom, truth, and the basic tenents
of living a meaningful life, this book will teach you to

- reconsider your priorities in light of God's love;
- rethink how you spend your time and money;
- focus on building meaningful and healthy relationships;
- reject the dizzying pursuit of fame and prestige;
- seek self-worth in relationship with God; and
- serve God in the simplest way: by loving others.

**"There is profound wisdom in this unassuming
book. I highly recommend it to anyone
who is longing for greater fulfillment in life."**
—Bob Schuchts
Author of *Be Healed*